T0034962

Praise for
Retirement Watch

"If there was a Mount Rushmore for retirement planning, Bob Carlson would be included. In my opinion, Bob is the #1 resource in the U.S. for factual and clear information on all things retirement, and his publications are must-reads for anyone who is serious about his specific retirement plan. For the over ten thousand Baby Boomers hitting age sixty-five every single day, this book should be required reading. It's that good."
   —**Stan The Annuity Man**

"For all those of you who fear running out of money after you retire, Bob Carlson's new book is the perfect antidote and will give you the freedom to enjoy your sunset years to the fullest."
   —**Mark Skousen,** editor of the Forecasts & Strategies newsletter and author of *The Maxims of Wall Street*

"During his almost three decades of leadership as chairman of the Fairfax County (VA) Employees' Retirement System, Bob Carlson has been at the forefront of innovative thinking on portfolio construction and implementation. His insights on markets and the interplay between economic growth and the forces of a potential new age of inflationary pressures hold real value to any retirement portfolio in the challenging times that lie ahead."
   —**Andrew J. Spellar,** CIO of Fairfax County (VA) Employees' Retirement System

"When it comes to assimilating the complexities of retirement and estate planning, there is no one better than Bob Carlson. Whether you're the data driven engineer or the financial planning novice, Bob has a gift for breaking down each aspect in depth to the degree that potential retirees at all levels of financial acumen will enjoy. *Retirement Watch* is a must-have instruction manual for all future and current retirees."
   —**Todd Phillips,** president of Estate Planning Specialists

"In today's complex financial universe, rife with new federal regulations and tax laws, it is nice to have an up-to-date guide that will steer us in the right direction. Bob's new book is precisely what the title says it is, an 'Essential Guide to Retiring,' for all of us, right here and now. As in all his works, including his prolific newsletter, Retirement Watch, Bob has a unique ability to translate confusion into easily understood English, with practical solutions. I will be recommending this 'Bible' to my clients for years to come. Thanks, Bob!"

—**David T. Phillips,** CEO of Estate Planning Specialists and author of *Estate Planning Made Easy* and *Disinherit the IRS*

Retirement Watch

Retirement Watch

The Essential Guide to Retiring in the 2020s

Bob Carlson

America's #1 Retirement Expert

REGNERY
CAPITAL
Washington, D.C.

Copyright © 2023 by Bob Carlson

All rights reserved. No part of this publication may be reproduced or transmitted in any form or by any means electronic or mechanical, including photocopy, recording, or any information storage and retrieval system now known or to be invented, without permission in writing from the publisher, except by a reviewer who wishes to quote brief passages in connection with a review written for inclusion in a magazine, newspaper, website, or broadcast.

Regnery® is a registered trademark and its colophon is a trademark of Salem Communications Holding Corporation

Regnery Capital is a trademark of Salem Communications Holding Corporation

Cataloging-in-Publication data on file with the Library of Congress

ISBN: 978-1-68451-333-8
eISBN: 978-1-68451-392-5

Published in the United States by
Regnery Capital, an Imprint of
Regnery Publishing
A Division of Salem Media Group
Washington, D.C.
www.Regnery.com

Manufactured in the United States of America

10 9 8 7 6 5 4 3 2

Books are available in quantity for promotional or premium use. For information on discounts and terms, please visit our website: www.Regnery.com.

In memory of my parents, Ed and Muriel,
and
to Elaine, my wife and best friend

CONTENTS

PREFACE

Retirement has changed, and it will change again.

After more than thirty years of researching, writing, and advising on retirement and retirement planning, I've learned that almost everything about retirement finances changes over time. As the sign on my high school chemistry teacher's desk read, "The only constant is change."

The pace of change seems to have increased in recent years, and significant changes seem to happen more often. More importantly, it appears we're entering a period of explosive changes in retirement finance. In Chapter 1 I describe a series of significant and rapidly occurring changes that I see coming. Any and all of these could affect your retirement finances in the coming years.

Because of the cumulative effects of these changes, the middle of this decade is going to be an especially tough time to retire, or to be in the early years of retirement.

But I don't write to cause panic or despair. I'm not a believer in the widely promoted "retirement crisis" or "retirement tsunami" discussed in the media. I don't intend to cause people to wring their hands, gnash their teeth, or rend their garments.

My goal is to help you get ahead of these changes so that you can increase your financial security and independence at a time when others are worrying. I believe that there are solutions and responses to the concerns that I have identified. By solutions I don't mean dramatic actions by Congress or regulators, though some such actions would help. Rather, I present practical actions that you can take, and I discuss them in clear and easy-to-understand terms. This is what I've been doing for more than thirty years in my newsletter Retirement Watch and its accompanying web site. I identify the issues and challenges facing retirees and pre-retirees and the changes that are occurring that might affect them.

From my independent research and analysis, I develop solutions and recommendations for my readers. I don't work for a major financial services firm, and I'm not selling my services. I work for my readers. I conduct my own independent research and study the results of other independent researchers. Then, I present my best analysis and conclusions to my readers. I understand that the best solution for one reader won't necessarily be appropriate for another. I don't believe in cookie-cutter financial advice. I try to explain who should consider one action and who should consider another.

I sometimes refer to what I do as "revving up your retirement." There are many parts and angles to your retirement finances. Too many retirees narrow their focus, dealing with only a few issues, especially their investments. In the last couple of decades they've relied on investment returns to carry the load of financial security, and healthy investment returns may have covered up mistakes and oversights in other areas. But your retirement will be more secure if you take a comprehensive approach. Over time, you should look at all the elements of your financial world and tweak as many parts as you can. When you complete your financial tune-up, your retirement will be sound and secure—the equivalent of a smooth-running engine. Instead of worrying about moves in the stock markets, you can be confident that whatever happens in the markets won't matter that much to you.

Don't try to take on everything at once. People who do that tend to become overwhelmed and give up. Work on one or two issues at a time. As you make decisions and take action you'll realize that you're becoming more financially secure and that you have fewer worries. You'll also be planning wisely for the changes headed our way.

Top young professional golfers have at least one trait in common—one you can benefit from even if you don't play golf. In interviews given in 2022, many of them said they had the same essential approach to golf: they never set out to become the top-rated golfer, to win a certain number of tournaments, nor to achieve accomplishments of that nature. Instead, they work each day to become a better golfer. That was their daily goal, and they often achieved it by making small improvements. They worked steadily at making those small improvements and over time, they became excellent golfers and reached significant milestones.

You need to take the same approach to your retirement planning, whether you're already retired or a pre-retiree. Work on your total game but only work on one or a few parts at a time. Work at it steadily. Seek advice from independent sources that rely on research instead of rules of thumb, or one-size-fits-all recommendations.

Crucially, always be on the alert for changes and potential changes, and be ready to adjust and adapt your plan as needed. Don't think that once a plan is developed that it's set in stone. Too often I run into people who say, "Well, I've been retired for a few years now.

There's not much I can do." That's a dangerous way of thinking. You always need to be looking out for factors that could upend your current plan. Such changes have been happening regularly, and they are likely to happen more frequently in the coming years.

By following these guidelines, you can have the retirement you desire, despite all the obstacles and difficulties facing retirees.

CHAPTER 1

The Coming Retirement Squeeze:
Why the Mid-2020s Will Be a Tough Time for Many Retirees

The mid-2020s could be the most challenging time in generations to be retired or approaching retirement. To be sure, there have been difficult periods in the past but challenges are emerging that are likely to present stiffer tests for this generation of retirees.

The last forty years have been generally favorable to retirees. There were tough periods within those four decades, but the overall trends have been good ones. Strong bull markets in both stocks and bonds began in August 1982. Government policies in the United States and in most of the developed world fostered an environment that has been favorable to economic growth and investment markets, and that has rewarded retirees. Investment returns over this period have been well above average, and that's despite at least two periods of significant and sustained losses in U.S. stock indices between 1982 and 2021. Strong investment returns covered up many of the mistakes people had made in other areas of their retirement finances.

That was the past, but many people now take for granted the environment that created those good results. They have been taking it for granted that inflation and interest rates would remain low, that monetary policy would support stock prices, that government policies would be favorable to businesses and investors, and that the other key characteristics of the recent past would be permanent.

That's not likely to be the case in the mid-2020s and beyond.

Many of those positive trends and policies that began in 1982 are ending. In addition, there are new, negative trends occurring that make the coming years likely to be very different from the previous forty years. In many ways, the coming years are more likely to resemble the 1970s than any other modern period, but this time there will be new and unique challenges.

Inflation Is Back

Inflation steadily increased after World War II and accelerated in the 1960s and 1970s. Inflation was so high and persistent that most individuals and businesses assumed it would continue indefinitely. They built that belief into their financial decision-making. That belief reinforced inflation and embedded it in the economy.

In 1982, the Federal Reserve (the Fed) made a significant change in its policies and set a new goal: wringing inflation out of the economy. It did that by raising interest rates and tightening monetary policy. The effort was successful, triggering a steady decline in inflation. After 1996, the 12-month increase in the Consumer Price Index (CPI) rarely rose above 2.5 percent, and it was often below 2 percent.

Other trends also contributed to lower inflation. Free trade and globalization expanded in the 1980s and boomed in the following years. As a result, the cost of manufacturing many goods decreased while supplies increased. At the same time, technology and other innovations increased productivity. Businesses were able to provide more goods and services at a lower cost than in the past. Deregulation and lower taxes also reduced the cost of doing business.

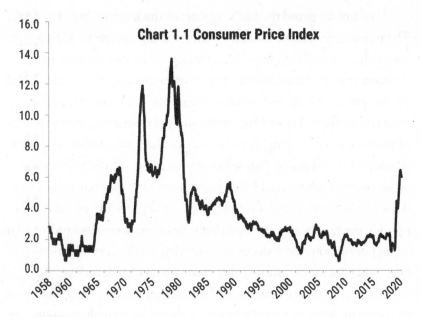

The Consumer Price Index since 1958. *All charts in this book were created by Robert Carlson using data published by the U.S. government.*

With inflation contained, the Fed was able to focus on supporting the economy and stock markets. After the financial crisis in 2007 and 2008, the Fed injected a great deal of liquidity into the economy and markets without having to worry about inflation. In fact, one of the Fed's stated goals after the financial crisis was to support the prices of stocks and other investments. The Fed believed that higher asset prices would increase the wealth of households and make them more likely to spend money and support economic growth, a phenomenon known as the wealth effect.

It became so clear that the Fed would inject money into the economy and markets whenever stock prices declined more than a modest amount that many investors dubbed the practice "the Fed Put," a term derived from the options markets. This popular expression demonstrates that investors were secure in the knowledge that the Fed would not allow stock indices to decline too far before acting to support them.

Low inflation and the Fed's support of stock prices ended in 2022. The massive fiscal and monetary stimulus during the Covid-19 pandemic dramatically increased the amount of money flowing through the economy. At the same time, key changes around the world reduced the supply of goods and services. Geopolitical conflicts, and some military conflicts, limited free trade and the positive economic effects of globalization. Aging populations in the United States and the developed world mean that a lower percentage of the population is active in the work force. This reduced supply of labor has forced businesses to increase compensation in an attempt to attract workers to provide the goods and services that consumers were demanding. An aging population also reduces productivity, and high productivity had been a key factor containing inflation in previous decades.

All of the money that the Fed injected in the economy increased the demand for goods and services at the same time that supplies of goods and services were declining. The result was higher prices and higher inflation. The Consumer Price Index reached its highest levels in forty years during 2022, with the twelve-month inflation rate exceeding 9 percent.

It is risky for retirees to assume that higher inflation is temporary. In fact it is likely that some level of higher inflation is embedded into the economy, and it will likely take some time to remove inflation expectations from households and businesses. The labor shortage is likely to be durable and can only be resolved with higher wages. In addition, trade conflicts and geopolitical tensions seem likely to be long-lasting. Greater regulation and higher taxes also seem likely to continue. In short most of the trends that led to the steady decline in inflation after 1982 seem to have stopped or reversed. Because of the changes in these major trends, retirees and those planning for retirement should expect the next five to ten years to differ in important ways from the preceding forty years.

Expect Lower Investment Returns

During the bull market that began in 1982, the rate of return on stock indexes greatly exceeded the rate of growth in the economy. That's unusual. Over the long term, stock prices should increase only as much as the economy does. The stock of an individual company can increase more than the economy, because the company might be taking business from other companies or might be in a sector of the economy that's growing faster than the overall economy. But the major stock indices shouldn't be able to sustain a long-term growth rate significantly higher than the rate of economic growth.

Yet in the last couple of decades stock index returns exceeded economic growth by a significant amount. The reasons for that excess return in stocks can be identified by examining the forces behind the excess growth rate. This leads us to the conclusion that the excess stock returns will not continue.

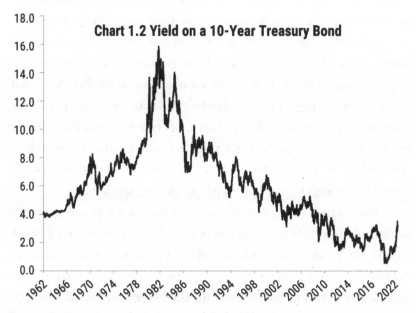

Interest rates on 10-Year U.S. Treasury bonds since 1962

Interest rates are key to the returns in bonds. A bond pays a fixed interest-rate to the bond owner. When market interest rates increase, an existing bond is less valuable to the investor because it's paying an interest rate lower than current market rates, so the value of the bond is reduced. But when interest rates decline, an existing bond is more valuable because its yield is higher than market rates and also higher than yields on new bonds. Steadily declining interest rates are why bonds generated very high returns after 1982. Existing bonds became more valuable to investors as rates declined.

Interest rates tend to decline while the economy is in a recession as well as when inflation is declining. Interest rates began hitting a series of historic lows after the financial crisis of 2007–2008, but interest rates are likely to increase when inflation is rising and when it is embedded in the economy. Unless the deflation of 2020 returns, interest rates won't return to their lows of 2020–2021 and could very well climb back to their historic averages. A rise to historic average interest rates or even higher rates would cause significant losses to bond investors.

Stock prices also are affected by interest rates. A stock is a risky asset, while a short-term Treasury bond is considered a risk-free asset. An investor is unlikely to buy a stock unless he or she believes it will deliver a higher return than a short-term Treasury bond. The difference between the expected return on a risk-free asset and the expected return on a risky asset such as a stock is known as the risk premium. An investor will buy a stock only if the return exceeds the risk-free return by enough to justify the risk, in the investor's view.

That's why when interest rates increase, stock prices generally decline. As interest rates rise, newly issued, risk-free Treasury bonds pay higher yields. Stock prices will then decline to ensure that the expected returns to buyers of stocks are high enough above the returns on risk-free bonds to compensate for the higher risk of the stock. So higher interest rates mean that, all other things being equal, the price of stocks declines. The riskier the stock, the more the price should decline when interest rates rise.

We saw this process in action in the first half of 2022. Interest rates on Treasury bonds steadily increased. The yield on the ten-year Treasury bond was 1.52 percent on December 31, 2021. It rose to 3.49 percent on June 14, 2022. That's a significant increase, and it triggered declines in stock prices. The S&P 500 stock index declined by more than 20 percent from the beginning of 2022 to mid-June 2022. The riskier Nasdaq 100 Index declined by more than 30 percent during the same period. Those declines in stock indices mostly reflected revaluing stock prices due to higher interest rates.

Low and steadily declining interest rates were a key factor in the bull market in stocks that began in 1982. As interest rates declined, investors were willing to pay higher prices for stocks. Those low interest rates were artificially induced by aggressive Fed

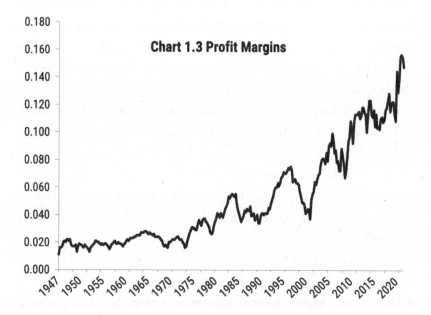

Chart 1.3 Profit Margins

U.S. corporate profit margins since 1947, in billions of dollars monetary policy. Without a significant economic downturn those low rates aren't likely to be repeated. If a higher rate of inflation is sustained, higher interest rates will also be sustained, and that will hurt stock returns.

Profit margins also boosted stock returns during the bull market. Several trends allowed publicly traded businesses to increase their profit margins over the years.

Key sectors of the economy came to be dominated by a small number of companies. Those businesses benefited from economies of scale, allowing them to provide their goods and services at lower costs than would be possible if they were smaller. Improvements in technology also led to higher productivity over the last few decades. Higher productivity improves profit margins.

In addition, the labor market was previously more favorable to employers. Employers generally had their choice of employees and didn't have to compete for them by offering higher compensation. Before 2020, average wages generally increased at a rate no higher than the CPI and often increased at a lower rate. A decline in the percentage of workers belonging to labor unions during this period also helped employers reduce costs.

Other factors, such as deregulation, globalization of trade, inventory management strategies, and lower corporate taxes, also contributed to higher profit margins.

By most measures profit margins and business profits increased at a rapid rate. Profit margins generally hit record levels, and the share of corporate revenues and earnings that went to labor declined.

The factors that led to increased profit margins and earnings during the last twenty years appear to be either peaking or in decline. These factors include low interest rates, low taxes, a weak labor market, globalization, free trade, deregulation, and industry

U.S. corporate profits since 1947, in dollars

concentration. An investor would be wise not to bet on a continued increase in profit margins or even that recent profit margins will be sustained.

Valuations placed on stocks were another reason stock prices increased much faster than the economy over the last few decades.

Stock valuations increase when investors are willing to pay more for each dollar of profit—for two reasons. One reason for this is if the investors expect the profits to increase rapidly. The other reason is if interest rates have declined and investors expect them to decline further. I believe that most of the increase in stock prices in the decades before 2022 was the result of both increases in profit margins and lower interest rates. Many analysts also point to earnings growth, but much of that higher earnings growth was the result of higher profit margins.

If you believe that interest rates will remain low and profit margins will continue to increase then you can conclude that stock returns will continue to be higher than the rate of economic growth. But that is not necessarily a safe approach.

The bottom line is that the new trends make it unlikely that investors will continue to pay more for each dollar of business profit, so stock valuations are unlikely to continue increasing. In fact they are likely to decline.

Another factor to consider is the natural rotation of the investment markets. U.S. stocks, especially U.S. growth stocks, were the dominant investment asset in the period following the financial crisis of 2007–2008, outpacing returns from other investments by significant margins. It is rare for the investment that had the dominant returns for a ten-year period to repeat as the top performer or even to be among the top performers over the next decade. Most often, there is a "return to the mean" in which long-term balance is restored when the previous decade's top performer begins to lag.

Many retirement plans are built on an assumption that future investment returns will be similar to those of the recent past. That could be dangerous. Periods of above-average investment returns (bull markets) tend to be followed by periods of below-average returns (bear markets). As I've explained previously, key factors supporting the long bull markets in stocks and bonds that began in 1982 appear to be fading or reversing. Retirees and pre-retirees planning for the next five to ten years should consider this change in trends carefully. They should be prepared for a "lost decade" or longer in stocks—such as we saw from the late 1960s through 1982 and from 2000 through about 2013.

For details about the potential for a long period of low investment returns and how to respond to that risk, see chapters 2, 6, and 14 below.

Financial Foundations Are Crumbling

Two programs are the financial foundation of virtually every retirement plan in the United States: Social Security and Medicare. Those two programs have been becoming less and less secure each year, and this trend has been going on for many years. The deteriorating conditions are no secret. The trustees of each program issue a detailed annual report on the financial condition of the programs, including projections for the next seventy-five years.

Medicare is the primary source of medical insurance for Americans who are age sixty-five or older. This program doesn't rely heavily on its trust fund. Most of the expenses of Medicare are supported by premiums from beneficiaries and general tax revenues. Only Part A, the hospital insurance segment of the program, relies on the trust fund. (See chapter 7 for details about Medicare and its different parts.)

The 2022 report from the trustees projected that the trust fund for Medicare Part A would be insolvent by 2028. Over the decade beginning in 2022, the trustees project Part A will run a deficit of $530 billion. A tax increase of 0.7 percent of payroll or a spending reduction of 15 percent, or a combination of the two, is needed to make the program solvent.

That's the conservative projection, assuming the program doesn't change much. But the Medicare Chief Actuary provided an alternative scenario in the same annual report. In this scenario, it is assumed that Congress periodically increases the rates paid to medical service providers to ensure many providers continue to accept Medicare beneficiaries. Under that assumption, the hospital insurance fund shortfall would be 1.6 percent of payroll instead of 0.7 percent, and the total spending would grow to 8.6 percent of GDP by 2096.[1]

Social Security is in worse shape because it relies on its trust fund to provide more of its funding. In its 2022 report the Board of Trustees of Social Security estimated the retirement trust fund will last until 2034, one year longer than was estimated in 2021. While the pandemic recession in 2020 was worse than anything the trustees had anticipated in previous annual reports, the recession was very short, and the recovery was much stronger than anticipated in the 2021 annual report.

When the trust fund is depleted, the Social Security retirement program won't end. The trustees estimated that the annual tax revenue coming into the program will be enough to pay about 77 percent of benefits indefinitely. That means if Congress doesn't take action to shore up the program before 2035, there will have to be an across-the-board reduction in benefits of 23 percent in 2035 and later years.

The trustees said that to keep the trust fund fully solvent through the next seventy-five years, in 2022 there would need to be a payroll tax increase of 3.24 percentage points, bringing the total payroll tax to 15.64 percent, or else a 20.3 percent reduction in scheduled benefits applied to all current and future beneficiaries or a 24.1 percent cut (if the reductions were applied only to those who initially become eligible for benefits in 2022 or later)—or some combination of the above.

Every year that reforms are delayed increases the extent of the required changes. For example, if changes aren't made until 2035, payroll taxes would have to increase 4.07 percentage points, to 16.47 percent, or else all benefits would have to decline by 24.9 percent, or some combination of the two.

But the assumptions that were used to arrive at the conclusions in the 2022 report from the Social Security trustees may be too optimistic. The program could be in worse shape than indicated.

For example, the report estimated that the annual cost of living adjustment (COLA) in benefits in 2023 would be only 3.8 percent, when the CPI for 2022 was already above 9 percent. The Chief Actuary of Social Security publicly contradicted that portion of the report shortly after it was issued, stating that the COLA for 2023 could be around 8 percent. The report also assumed unrealistically low COLAs for the years following.

The trustees also assumed that the birth rate in the U.S. would increase to 2.0 births per woman beginning in 2021. More births would mean more workers in the workforce and more taxes flowing into the system. That would improve the system's financial condition. But the birth rate assumption contradicts both recent experience and forecasts from sources specializing in demographics.

The conclusion that retirees and pre-retirees should draw is that changes in Social Security and Medicare are likely and necessary. The longer Congress waits to address this the more severe the reforms are likely to be. Retirement plans need flexibility and should have a cushion to adjust to benefits and tax changes.

There's a good possibility that those already retired or within a few years of retirement won't be affected by some of these changes. They'll be grandfathered into the current program while later retirees bear the burden of cuts. That's what happened with the Social Security reforms of the early 1980s. But retirees with higher incomes and wealth might not be grandfathered. They should be prepared for additional means-testing that imposes higher costs or provides lower benefits on them.

One Way or Another, We'll Pay for Excess Debt

Debt can be destructive.

Federal debt was already high before the financial crisis, but it increased rapidly from 2007–2008 onward. Federal debt increased dramatically again during the Covid-19 pandemic. But official federal debt isn't the only obligation the government has. The federal government has many other types of obligations and pseudo-obligations that aren't officially listed as debt, such as veterans' benefits, loan guarantees, Social Security, Medicare, Medicaid, and more. All told, these obligations amount to trillions of dollars.

The debt needs to be paid back over time through some combination of inflation, taxes, and reduced spending on other items. In addition, though they disagree on the details, economists agree that when a national government's debt level exceeds a certain percentage of gross domestic product (GDP), the debt burden reduces economic growth. The level of the U.S. government's debts and other obligations is well past that point, and most economists agree.

The United States has managed to delay the negative consequences of the high level of debt issued by the federal government after the financial crisis because the Federal Reserve bought a high percentage of the debt. That debt-buying program injected extra money into the economy and markets, leading to the high inflation that began in 2022. The Fed is unlikely to resume that kind of debt-buying any time soon. A consequence is that the federal debt burden could soon start restraining economic growth.

There are also other debts to worry about. Many state and local governments have high debt levels as well as obligations that aren't formally considered debt. Employee pension benefits are a major obligation of state and local governments. The unfunded employee pension liabilities are so high for some states and localities that it's difficult to see how the governments will ever pay them.

High levels of government debt will affect your retirement both indirectly and directly.

The reduction in economic growth from the excess debt is likely to result in lower investment returns. In addition, governments are likely to reduce services over time as they struggle to pay their debts. That will require you to either forego the services, or pay separately for them. The high levels of debt also mean that your taxes are likely to increase over time. Taxes are imposed at all levels of government. Unlike the federal government, most state and local governments can't run budget deficits indefinitely. They must reduce spending or increase taxes. Either way, high government debt is likely to cost you more during the retirement years.

Global Politics and Increasing Conflict

The fall of the Soviet Union and the end of the Cold War were assumed by many to be the beginning of an era of reduced global conflict. But the period of reduced conflict didn't last long. In the last few years, conflicts seem to have increased, reversing some of the trends that had improved economic conditions in previous decades, such as globalization and free trade. Conflicts between governments tend to reduce economic growth and disrupt investment markets in coming years.

I'm not an expert on global politics, but it's easy to see that some things have changed. Both Russia and China have decided to challenge the United States for global leadership. The challenges won't necessarily involve military conflict, though it is certainly possible. Short of that, we could see trade and travel restrictions, targeted regulations, cyber-attacks, and other disruptions. Global conflicts and tensions are likely to be a more important factor in the economy and markets than they were in the recent past.

The geopolitical tensions may also lead to internal political problems in developed countries, including the United States. In the developed countries, there has been a rise in nationalism on both the left and right sides of the political spectrum. That makes it harder to resolve global conflicts. There are also fewer areas of agreement than in the past between people in different political parties within countries. Those trends make it harder for elected officials to agree on solutions to national problems. Civil unrest also seems to have increased in many countries, including the United States.

Economic conflicts and hostility to wealthier people in society are also growing. We could see those conflicts play out in a range of actions, from personal attacks to legislation targeting select groups.

These and other conflicts within and between nations will likely reduce economic growth below what it would have been without the conflicts, and that will reduce investment returns. The conflicts, especially the global conflicts, are also likely to cause higher federal government spending and taxes, which, as we have seen, could also threaten retirement in a variety of ways.

The Boomer Peak and Its Consequences

The population is aging, and that's a problem.

The Baby Boomers have triggered massive changes in institutions and the economy as well as significant disruptions in society throughout their lives. Now, most of that generation—those born from 1946 to 1964—is in or nearing the retirement years. The first Boomers reached age sixty-five in 2011. Since then, about ten thousand Boomers per day have turned sixty-five. But that is only the beginning. The middle section of the Boomer generation, which is larger than the early section, will begin turning sixty-five in 2024. At that point an estimated twelve thousand people will be turning sixty-five every day. That's the Boomer Peak. All Boomers, an estimated 73 million people, will have reached age sixty-five by 2030. One-fifth of the U.S. population will be sixty-five or older in 2030. There will be more sixty-five-year-olds than children in that year.

The pressure on every aspect of retirement will increase as the Boomer Peak approaches, and it will continue as long as a significant portion of the boomers are with us. Additional demands will be put on institutions, programs, and sectors of the economy affected by whatever age group the Boomers are in at the moment, just as they were when the Boomers were young. The Boomers crowded schools and universities during their early years, as they went through their life cycle, they increased the demand for housing, baby products, and more. Now, they're putting stress on goods and services demanded by those aged sixty-five and over.

The primary stress is on Social Security and Medicare, as we saw above. But the Boomers are also straining medical care. There are shortages of doctors, nurses, and other medical providers as well as of medical supplies. These shortages will only become worse, making it harder to schedule appointments for medical care and also increasing the cost.

In short, many of the goods and services you need and desire during retirement are likely to be in short supply and increase in price because of the aging Boomers.

As we have seen, an aging population also means decreased productivity and economic growth. This is a global problem. While the U.S. population is aging, its population is much younger than the populations of the developed nations of Europe and Japan. China also has a very old population, a result of the one-child birth policy it adopted several decades ago and relaxed only recently. The aging global population, especially in the major economies of the world, is another reason to expect economic growth to be lower than it has been the last few decades.

What You Should Do: Rev Up Your Retirement Plan

Most of the trends following 1982 favored retirees. But those trends are peaking and reversing and are likely to be against you if you will be retired during the mid-2020s, especially if you begin your retirement during that period. They're being succeeded by new trends that will make it more difficult to maintain financial security and independence during retirement.

But my message is not one of despair and giving up. My message is that you can have financial security and independence in retirement, but you can't rely on the strategies and systems that worked for previous generations of retirees. Those retirees benefited from low inflation, low interest rates, high investment returns, and a bull market. All of these trends are likely to alter significantly.

Instead, this is a time to rev up your retirement planning. The big trends will no longer cover up retirement mistakes and oversights. When most people think of retirement planning, they think first of the investment markets and how to increase returns. I'm saying you should pay more attention to the other elements of your retirement finances. You can't do much about the investment markets; you certainly can't control or predict them. But there are other aspects of your retirement finances that you can control. Collectively they're going to have a big impact on your retirement financial security.

Rev up your retirement planning by adding more protection to your finances. Fortify your retirement by paying attention to all the steps in the rest of this book.

The actions you take now and in the next few years will determine how vulnerable you are and how likely you are to be buffeted by these challenging new trends.

CHAPTER 2

How to Build a Moat around Your Retirement

Retirees are likely to face some fierce headwinds in the mid-2020s and beyond. The risks to your financial security and independence in retirement are real, but you don't have to fall prey to the forces and trends described in chapter 1. I didn't describe those risks simply to frighten readers. I described them to urge you to take actions that will increase your financial security and independence. There are many factors affecting your retirement finances that you can't control. But many decisions are under your control, and the choices you make can protect you and your family from the forces and trends that threaten retirement security.

While the details of retirement plans vary between individuals, there are concerns, risks, and fears common to most retirees. There also are broad strategies and actions most retirees should take to counter those risks. I refer to these strategies collectively as building a moat around your retirement to protect you from the forces that threaten your security. Establishing a moat allows you to spend more time doing the things you really want to do in retirement and less time worrying about spending too much, running out of money, or having your financial security upended by outside forces.

The terms "moat" may seem defensive, but the actions I describe here can also be viewed as offensive or affirmative steps to enhance your retirement. They are ways to rev up or amp up your retirement. Taking these actions will put you in better position than those who are more passive about their retirement planning, leaving themselves vulnerable to change and outside forces.

In this chapter I describe the key steps you should take to increase financial security and establish the retirement you desire. In the rest of the book, I provide more details on each of these steps, as well as other actions you can take to ensure your retirement security and financial independence.

Establish Your Retirement Paycheck

The prime goal of all the saving and investing you did during the working years was to turn the accumulated capital into a lifetime cash flow, or a retirement paycheck. The nest egg is there to fund your desired standard of living and to last for the rest of your life, no matter how long that might be. In effect, you want to replace the paycheck that was received during the working years with a steady, reliable paycheck from your portfolio and savings.

It has always been easy to find advice on how to accumulate money for retirement. But when I began researching, writing, and advising about retirement finances more than thirty years ago I was among the few considering the best ways to turn that retirement savings into income and cash flow. Fortunately, there's been a lot of research done in recent years into what many financial professionals now call the "decumulation" period of life. Even so, many enter retirement without a clear plan for turning their savings into lifetime income. More importantly, they aren't confident that they have the tools to ensure their nest eggs will last for the rest of their lives.

The first step in creating that lifetime cash flow is to establish a stream of guaranteed lifetime income. When you have guaranteed lifetime income, you're ensured of not running out of money during retirement. Almost everyone has at least one source of guaranteed lifetime income—Social Security. This source of guaranteed lifetime income also has the benefit of being indexed for inflation. But you can also convert some of your retirement savings into additional guaranteed lifetime income.

In chapter 3 I explain the key benefits of guaranteed lifetime income. The data shows that the more guaranteed lifetime income you have, the more money you'll be able to spend in retirement, and the less you'll worry about running out of money, volatility in the investment markets, and other concerns.

The first step in creating a retirement paycheck is maximizing your Social Security benefits. Most people don't claim their Social Security benefits at the optimum time, and they often regret their decision later in retirement. In chapter 4, I explain the factors to consider before claiming Social Security and how to determine the optimum time to claim, as well as the importance of spouses' coordinating their benefits decisions.

The next step is to determine how much, if any, of your nest egg to convert into guaranteed lifetime income. This is a personal decision that depends on the amount of risk you want to take, the amount of control you want, and your potential regret from missing opportunities in the markets. Most people have more satisfying and secure retirements when they receive enough guaranteed lifetime income to pay their regular or continuing expenses each month. This guaranteed lifetime income can be generated by converting a portion of the nest egg into an annuity. In chapter 5, I discuss the best ways to convert a portion of your nest egg into guaranteed lifetime income and the different kinds of income.

The final step in establishing your retirement paycheck is to develop a plan and process for converting your retirement investment portfolio into a regular stream of cash flow. You want to be able to spend your accumulated capital without taking the risk of running out of money later in retirement. To do this, develop an estimate of how much money you're likely to spend to maintain the retirement lifestyle you desire. In chapter 6 I present data on how retirees typically spend their money over time and show you how to establish a process for distributing money from the nest egg to fund your desired standard of living while avoiding the risk of running out of money in retirement.

Converting your retirement savings into a reliable retirement paycheck or lifetime cash flow is a key step to protecting your retirement security from the headwinds that retirees will face during the rest of the 2020s.

Minimize Out-of-Pocket and Surprise Medical Expenses

Spending on medical services increases as we age. Many pre-retirees and retirees worry that they will incur high out-of-pocket medical expenses that will deplete their nest eggs during retirement. Fueling these fears are estimates issued annually that regularly show that a retired married couple is likely to spend $300,000 or more in out-of-pocket on medical expenses over the next thirty years.

To avoid the risk of having medical expenses drain your retirement nest egg, you need to avoid the Medicare mistakes many beneficiaries make.

You must first decide whether you want to join a Medicare Advantage plan or stay with original Medicare. In chapter 7 I explain the differences between the two options and guide you toward making the best decision for you. If you opt for original Medicare you should also purchase additional medical insurance. In chapter 7 I also explain what kind of insurance you need and how to shop for the policy or policies that are best for you.

Making good choices about Medicare substantially reduces the risk that you'll have significant out-of-pocket medical expenses or surprise medical bills during retirement. You could save some money in the short term by opting for lower insurance premiums, but most people save more in the long term by following guidelines that will limit the potential for high out-of-pocket expenses, as explained in chapter 7.

Position Your Portfolio for Both Growth and Protection

Retirees must make these important investment decisions for themselves since fewer and fewer employees have employer pensions. They enter retirement with substantial investment portfolios in 401(k) plans or IRAs.

You can't control the markets or have any influence over them. But you can position an investment portfolio to earn solid returns and to protect most of the principal from the effects of major stock market declines.

Many factors affect what investment markets do in the short term. You can't anticipate short-term market changes and shouldn't attempt to. Over intermediate- and long-term periods, however, two economic forces influence what happens in the market. These factors are economic growth and inflation. Sometimes both factors move in the same

Chart 2.1 The Four Potential Phases of the Economic or Market Cycle

Rising Growth, Falling Inflation **Expansion**	**Peak** Rising Growth, Rising Inflation
Trough Falling Growth, Falling Inflation	**Contraction** Falling Growth, Rising Inflation

The four phases of the typical economic cycle

direction, and at other times they move in different directions. As a result, there are four potential phases during a full economic or market cycle. These phases are shown in Chart 2-1.

The phases are the different stages of the typical economic cycle. While there can be differences between economic cycles and short-term variations in any given phase, over time a clear pattern emerges. The cycle begins with the expansion phase. In an expansion, economic growth is rising while inflation is falling. Eventually, inflation begins to increase because of the forces of the expansion. The economy then moves into the peak phase in which economic growth continues to be positive while inflation is rising.

The Federal Reserve Bank usually begins the end of the peak phase by tightening monetary policy in order to reduce inflation. The economy enters the contraction phase when economic growth falls because of the tighter monetary policy. Inflation continues to rise because tighter monetary policy takes longer to affect inflation than economic growth. Finally, the economy enters the trough period when both economic growth and inflation are falling. Sometime during the trough, the Federal Reserve Bank decides the economy needs to be stimulated to end or avoid a recession. A stimulative monetary policy is initiated, and the cycle begins again with an increase in economic growth.

The cycle presents a difficulty for many retirees since they don't have portfolios that are genuinely diversified, though they think their portfolios are diversified and may even have been told so by a financial professional. A typical portfolio is about 60 percent invested in stocks and 40 percent invested in bonds. As someone approaches retirement, the stock allocation might be reduced, but it is still significant. In these portfolios, the returns and volatility are at least 90 percent correlated with the stock indices. That means the portfolio does well only during the expansion and peak phases of the cycle. Positive returns depend heavily on positive economic growth, and they aren't even particularly good when growth is rising if inflation is also.

This isn't a big problem for many investors. During the working years, the portfolio has years to recover from falling markets, and you're continuing to add new savings to the portfolio. But, as I explain in chapter 15, people in the period that includes the five years before and after retirement are susceptible to what's called sequence-of-returns risk. A decline in the portfolio during that period can disrupt a person's retirement plan.

The retirement nest egg is generally at or near its highest value as you near retirement. A significant decline in its value at that point greatly reduces the chance of success for the retirement plan. You no longer have years for the markets to recover and put your plan back on track. At the same time, after retirement you aren't adding new savings to the portfolio because you're no longer working. In fact, you are likely to begin withdrawing money from the portfolio to pay for retirement living expenses. The money withdrawn won't be in the portfolio, as it was during your working years, to benefit from the next market recovery. That means the portfolio must earn an even higher return after the decline to get back on track.

Even worse, sometimes the contraction and trough periods last longer than average. A retiree with a traditional portfolio would be greatly harmed by a long-term bear market that began just before or during the early years of retirement. As I explain in chapter 15, such periods occurred in the 1960s and 1970s, and also in the early 2000s. A retiree should be aware of this possibility and seek to protect the portfolio from such events. As I explained in chapter 1, there's a much higher probability than usual that the mid-2020s and beyond will be such a period.

One strategy is to have a portfolio that is more balanced than the traditional portfolio—one that includes more types of assets which do well in all the different economic environments. The traditional portfolio is heavily dependent on rising economic growth and the rising stock prices that accompany it. A more balanced portfolio won't do as well as the traditional portfolio during bull markets in stocks, but it will protect capital better during other phases of the market cycle. It is likely to avoid big losses and have more solid, steady returns over time. It can even generate positive returns when stocks are losing value.

The investments most likely to benefit from rising growth are stocks, corporate bonds, real estate, and commodities. When growth is falling, those assets are likely to be hurt. The investments that typically do well in an environment of declining growth are traditional bonds, inflation-indexed bonds, gold, and the dollar. Investments that usually do well when inflation is rising include real estate, commodities, inflation-indexed bonds, gold, and some foreign currencies. When inflation is falling, investments that do well include stocks, corporate bonds, and traditional bonds.

Having a more balanced portfolio is not the only way to protect yourself from bad periods in the markets.

Another strategy is to have a more tactical investment strategy instead of a fixed-asset allocation. Consider all the assets discussed above and how they perform in different phases of the market and economic cycle. As the phase of the cycle appears to be changing you can increase and decrease holdings of the appropriate assets. For example, when the economy appears to be shifting from the trough phase to the growth phase you could increase holdings of stocks, real estate, corporate bonds, and commodities and reduce holdings of government bonds, inflation-indexed bonds, and gold.

The tactical approach is more difficult to execute well. Many people confuse it with short-term trading, but the changes in the portfolio should be made infrequently. Only a major shift in economic growth or inflation should lead to a change in the portfolio. Most people shouldn't attempt to implement a tactical strategy on their own. They should use a financial advisor, invest in one or more funds that make the decisions, or make use of some other professional source of expertise.

The Federal Reserve Bank supported investment markets following the financial crisis of 2007–2008 and increased that support in 2020 during the pandemic. That support greatly boosted investment returns during that period, covering up numerous financial mistakes people had made. As I explained in chapter 1, retirees can't count on similar results in the coming years, and they should adjust their investment strategies accordingly.

The uncertainty and volatility of investment markets is another reason to consider repositioning some of your retirement savings as guaranteed lifetime income. Let the insurance companies that issue the annuities worry about what's happening in the investment markets while you collect monthly income payments.

Avoid the Retirement Tax Traps

Many people enter retirement with the idea that their taxes, especially their income taxes, will decline after they retire. These days that's often not the case. Congress knows that older Americans have most of the income and wealth so they make sure they still pay hefty taxes. Retirees need to be aware of two major tax threats to their retirement security.

One threat is what I call Stealth Taxes. Congress didn't want to enact higher tax rates specifically on retirees. Instead, it created a series of measures that increase income taxes as income rises without increasing the tax rate. The Stealth Taxes tend to be triggered when adjusted gross income (AGI) increases.

As AGI increases, Social Security benefits go from being completely tax free to having up to 85 percent of benefits included in gross income. In addition, the Medicare premium surtax causes a person's Medicare premium to rise from the base level that every beneficiary pays to a higher level, with the surtax increasing as AGI increases. These are only two examples but more details of the Stealth Taxes and how to reduce or avoid them are in chapter 10.

The other tax threat is the deferred tax burden on your traditional IRA and 401(k). Congress created tax incentives to encourage people to save money in these accounts, but the incentives only defer the taxes, they do not eliminate them. The deferrals operate like a mortgage on your IRA. You borrowed the money by not paying taxes when money was put in the account and as it earned investment returns. In retirement, those taxes have to be paid when money is distributed from the accounts. In addition, you'll be required to make distributions from the account even if you don't need the money. Plus, if you don't spend all the money in the accounts during your lifetime, your heirs will have to pay the taxes when they distribute money from the accounts.

The distributions might also increase your income enough to trigger or increase the Stealth Taxes. In addition, the mortgage on your IRA essentially charges interest by converting what could have been long-term capital gains or qualified dividends, if earned outside the IRA, into ordinary income when distributed from the account.

You really own only the after-tax value of the accounts, and your heirs inherit only the after-tax value. The taxes on retirement account accumulations may be onerous, especially if income tax rates increase in the future. If tax rates rise, you will have benefited from the tax breaks when tax rates were lower only to pay the income taxes when rates are higher. Tax rates are likely to rise in the future because of the heavy federal debt burden and the precarious financial position of both Social Security and Medicare. Many people instinctively want to defer distributions from the accounts for as long as possible, but that can also make their taxes higher: when distributions need to be made more money will have to be distributed.

You should try to maximize the after-tax value of IRAs and other retirement accounts. There are strategies that will increase the after-tax value available during your lifetime or to your heirs when they inherit the accounts. I discuss this in chapter 9, where I also lay out important rules and strategies that can increase the after-tax value of 401(k) accounts to help you avoid triggering penalties or taxes when moving them.

Have a Long-Term Care Plan

Nobody wants to need long-term care, but everyone should have a plan for where they want to receive the care and how it will be paid for if they need it. Unfortunately, few people even want to discuss the possibility of long-term care with their family, friends, or financial advisors.

Because few people want to talk about long-term care, misinformation and misunderstandings abound. You need to know the real data about the potential for needing long-term care, how long the need might last, and how much it can cost. I present the data in Chapter 8 so you can make informed decisions.

You might choose to purchase an insurance policy to help pay for any long-term care you need. Otherwise, long-term care expenses for you and your spouse could deplete your retirement assets and leave your heirs with little or no inheritance. There have been quite a few changes in the long-term care insurance marketplace in the last fifteen years, and in chapter 8 I discuss these changes, review the different types of insurance policies you should consider, and explain how to choose a policy that provides the type of coverage you need and can afford.

Expect and Prepare for Change

A retirement plan isn't fixed, like a road map. The plan is based on number of assumptions about the future, and also on current laws and other features of the retirement environment. But, as I've said, retirement has changed and will change again. Most of the factors affecting your plan as it is implemented will be different from what was originally anticipated. Some things will change in ways more favorable to you, while other changes will be adverse. Some changes will be small or gradual while others will be sudden and significant.

A retiree shouldn't expect a plan to be set in stone. A retirement plan is not something you can prepare and then forget about. You need to expect changes, be aware of the assumptions in your plan, and then be on the lookout for changes that should trigger modifications in your strategies. Some people will monitor events on a regular basis, frequently searching for news and events that would warrant a review of their plans. Others will review plans less often. Every retiree should take some time at least once a year to review the plan and its assumptions about the future. You will need to determine if the plan should be modified because of things that have changed or seem likely to change. Examining your plan regularly will make it likelier that when adjustments are needed they will be fairly small and easy to manage. Waiting longer between reviews comes with the risk that when changes are needed, they will be significant.

You don't want to overreact. Some people follow the headlines closely and are inclined to make frequent, significant changes. For example, they want to change their investment positions based on the most recent moves in the markets or economy. They might want to overhaul their estate plans at the first rumor that Congress will make changes in estate taxes. Frequent and pre-emptive changes are not usually a good idea, and they shouldn't be necessary if you carefully consider your plan and develop your strategies. You should *expect* short-term disruptions, especially in the investment markets. I've known people who were inclined to overhaul their portfolios after each election, believing each election would lead to major, immediate changes in tax laws, investment markets, and more. Reacting in this way will not make for a satisfying or secure retirement. You need to be able to differentiate between short-term, temporary, and minor changes with longer-term and meaningful changes, and balance your approach accordingly.

After reviewing your plan and recent events, try to identify meaningful events and trends. Then, applying your review, determine changes that should be made in your plan and implement them.

CHAPTER 3

Why You Need Guaranteed Lifetime Income to Reduce Risk and Increase Spending

Many people do a good job of saving and investing for retirement. Then, when they reach retirement, they fail to take the next necessary step. They don't develop a good plan for turning the accumulated savings into income and cash flow. That failure is the source of much of the insecurity among retirees and pre-retirees, and it increases the probability a retirement plan will fail.

Running out of money is the prime worry of many retirees and near-retirees, for many reasons: major medical expenses, long-term care costs, or a bear market in stocks. Other key money worries are the possibilities of living a long time, having to help family members, and paying for future tax increases.

All of these fears are realistic. What's important is how you respond. The probability of running out of money in retirement can be reduced significantly by following practical steps. In other chapters of this book I explain how to develop a spending strategy for your retirement savings, how to minimize the potential for large out-of-pocket medical expenses or long-term care expenses, and how to manage other specific risks of retirement. But first, in this chapter, I explain the first step to building a fortress around your retirement that will make your nest egg last longer and allow you to spend more money during retirement than you otherwise could have, while reducing the probability that you may run out of money.

The Importance of Guaranteed Income

Guaranteed lifetime income used to be an essential element of most retirees' plans. Today, it's a neglected retirement planning tool. Yet having adequate guaranteed lifetime income significantly reduces the potential that you'll outlive your money in retirement. It should help overcome the money fears many people harbor over their retirement years. A bonus is that guaranteed lifetime income allows a retiree to safely increase spending in retirement. With guaranteed lifetime income the retiree will achieve the seemingly unreachable goal of being both more financially secure and able to spend more of the money saved for retirement.

A number of studies and analyses support the benefits of increasing guaranteed lifetime income.

A retiree who is concerned about having enough money to last through a long retirement should reconsider the asset allocation of his or her portfolio. The retiree can include a number of different assets in the portfolio, and he or she must decide how much to allocate to each asset class. The portfolio can include stocks, bonds, commodities, real estate, and other assets.

Most U.S. retirees' portfolios are dominated by stocks and bonds, or other fixed income investments. Stocks are chosen because they tend to offer the highest long-term returns. They can help the portfolios grow or at least maintain their purchasing power against inflation.

Bonds and other fixed income investments are owned primarily for two reasons: they generate steady income from interest payments, and they are less volatile than stocks. Their greater stability reduces fluctuations in the value of the portfolio over time and specifically reduces losses during bear markets in stocks.

But suppose the universe of potential assets is expanded to include sources of guaranteed lifetime income, such as a single-premium immediate annuity (SPIA). A SPIA pays a fixed amount of income to its owner on a regular basis (monthly, quarterly, or annually) for as long as the person lives, much like an employer pension. (SPIAs are discussed in more detail in chapter 5.)

A study published in the December 2001 issue of *The Journal of Financial Planning* looked at four different asset allocations and used a method known as Monte Carlo modeling to estimate which portfolios were most likely to last long enough to fund at least a thirty-year retirement, assuming 4.5 percent of the portfolio is distributed each year. The study found that putting 25 percent to 50 percent of the portfolio into SPIAs increased the probability it could sustain at least thirty years of retirement. The researchers compared the odds a portfolio would last more than thirty years when each portfolio contained different allocations to SPIAs, ranging from a 0 percent SPIA allocation to a 50 percent SPIA allocation. The portfolios compared ranged from a conservative portfolio in which only 20 percent was invested in stocks to an aggressive portfolio in which 85 percent was invested in stocks.

The conservative portfolio had only a 32.6 percent probability of success when it held no SPIAs. But the probability of success increased to 53.3 percent when SPIAs were 25 percent of the portfolio and 81.3 percent when SPIAs were 50 percent of the portfolio. The improvement was less dramatic for the aggressive portfolio, which started with a 90 percent probability of lasting at least thirty years when it contained no SPIAs, but the probability still increased when the 15 percent that was allocated to bonds or fixed income was switched over to SPIAs.[1]

One lesson is that investing aggressively throughout retirement is more likely to be successful than conservative investing—provided stocks at least match their long-term returns during your retirement. But that's not a given (see chapters 1, 6, and 20). That's why there was still a 10 percent probability of failure for the aggressive stock portfolio. And if a strong bull market preceded your retirement, returns are likely to be below their historic average in the years that immediately follow, when your retirement begins.

Another lesson is that regardless of the rest of your investment strategy, shifting some or all of the fixed income allocation to SPIAs decreases the probability of outliving your retirement nest egg, often substantially. After all, a SPIA promises to pay you regular income no matter how long you live. It's difficult to run out of money with that guarantee along with Social Security.

More recent research from several researchers builds on the earlier study and reenforces its findings. Key researchers are Wade Pfau, Michael Finke, Moshe Milevsky, and Peng Chen. For example, in an article in the February 2013 issue of *The Journal of Financial Planning*, Pfau concluded that SPIAs or some other type of guaranteed lifetime income should replace bonds and similar investments in retirement portfolios.[2] He titled an article he wrote for the website Advisor Perspectives, "Why Bond Funds Don't Belong in Retirement Portfolios." Compared to bonds, annuities that pay guaranteed lifetime income reduce risk and increase consumption during retirement.[3]

The higher the percentage of savings that is repositioned as guaranteed income, the higher the safe spending rate, according to a study by David M. Blanchett in the April 2017 *Journal of Financial*

Planning. According to Blanchett's study, the amount of guaranteed income is the most significant factor that should be considered in determining the safe spending rate, which is the maximum percentage of the nest egg that can be spent each year without taking the risk of depleting the nest egg during retirement. The concept of the safe spending rate is discussed in more detail in chapter 6.

Blanchett considered investment returns, asset allocation, and adjusting the annual withdrawals with changes in the portfolio's value. Blanchett assumed that the amount of guaranteed income increased with the Consumer Price Index, as happens with Social Security benefits and inflation-adjusted annuities.

Blanchett went through a range of scenarios using different economic and investment assumptions and found that the level of guaranteed income could change the safe spending rate by about four percentage points: the safe spending rate is about 6 percent of the portfolio's initial value when 95 percent of a household's wealth is in guaranteed income, but it declines to 2 percent of the investment portfolio when only 5 percent of the wealth is in guaranteed income. None of the other factors changed the safe spending rate as much.[4]

The Blanchett study demonstrated something that most of us understand intuitively. When all other things are equal, a household with $100,000 per year in guaranteed lifetime income can afford to spend a higher percentage of its nest egg each year than a household with only $10,000 of guaranteed income per year. The household with $100,000 of guaranteed lifetime income can spend that amount one year and be sure of receiving the same amount the following year. The household with less guaranteed income can't be sure of how much it will be able to spend the next year, because investment market fluctuations could change the value of its savings, and thus the amount of its annual income.

A SPIA or other source of guaranteed lifetime income eliminates longevity risk by guaranteeing a fixed amount of income will be paid regardless of how long a person lives. The risk of a long life is taken by the insurance company which spreads that risk across a large number of people. The insurance company will come out even if it has a large customer base with a life expectancy that matches the insurer's estimates. The retiree benefits from what are known as mortality credits. This simply means that the annuity owners who outlive average life expectancy benefit from the investments in annuities made by those who don't live to life expectancy.

Here's a simple example of how guaranteed lifetime income can generate better results than bonds or other fixed-income investments. A sixty-seven-year-old woman is retiring and has accumulated $500,000. She decides the entire amount will be put into either safe income investments (such as government bonds or bank certificates of deposit) or SPIAs. She plans to spend $2,800 monthly, or $33,600 annually, because that is how much income she would receive if the entire $500,000 were put into SPIAs.

Let's say that if the entire amount were put in safe income investments she'll earn 3 percent interest on the deposits annually. But if the $500,000 is earning 3 percent in safe income investments, she will receive only $15,000 annually, or $1,250 monthly in interest income. She'll have to draw down her principal each month to pay the rest of her expenses. Under this scenario, she'll run out of money around age eighty-six. If she wants the money to last longer, she will have to reduce her monthly spending or find a way to earn a higher return on her money. Earning the higher return would involve taking more investment risk. Whereas if she puts the entire $500,000 in SPIAs, she receives $2,800 monthly for as long as she lives with no investment or interest rate risk.[5]

It's important to note that none of the studies concludes that most people should put all or most of their assets into guaranteed lifetime income. Most people will want some assets in stocks or other growth-oriented assets to maintain purchasing power over time, to see their nest eggs increase in value if there's a bull market in stocks during their retirement years, and to leave some of their assets to their heirs.

Increase Your Spending—Safely

Another study looked at guaranteed lifetime income from another angle: how much money a retiree could or would spend based on the amount of retirement assets that were repositioned to generate guaranteed lifetime income.

How people hold or invest their wealth influences how much they spend, according to the paper, by David Blanchett and Michael Finke. They found that most retirees can increase their spending safely without increasing the risk of running out of money—something affirmed by the other studies. Blanchett and Finke went a step further and showed that retirees actually will increase their spending if a higher percentage of their assets is in guaranteed lifetime income.

Wealth is not the key determinant of the level of retirement spending, according to the paper. The form in which wealth is held is more of a determinant of spending levels. Retirees with more guaranteed lifetime income are likely to spend more money than those whose cash flow is derived primarily from investment portfolios, or other assets, and who have little or no guaranteed lifetime income.

This study is not mere theory. The authors used real data compiled over years from the University of Michigan Health and Retirement Study, a biannual survey of approximately twenty thousand Americans from age fifty until the end of their lives. The paper focused on people who had at least $100,000 in savings. The researchers compared how much people actually spent with how much they could safely spend. The "could spend" estimate was derived assuming a percentage of assets was used to buy guaranteed lifetime income and estimating the amount of income that would be generated, using data on the income annuities paid at the time the people in the survey reached age sixty-five. The key finding was that households with more wealth in guaranteed income spent significantly more each year than retirees who held more of their wealth in financial assets.

That's logical. A high percentage of retirees and pre-retirees are hesitant to spend down assets. They want to spend only income and gains or even to increase their net worth during retirement. They're still in the saving and accumulating mode of the pre-retirement years or are concerned a bear market will substantially reduce their savings. Also, very few retirees develop a systematic spending plan that includes spending down their assets, as discussed in chapter 6. The result is they spend less than they could.

The conclusion of the Blanchett and Finke research is that retirees will spend more per year in retirement if they shift some of their nest egg from financial assets into guaranteed lifetime income. Every dollar of financial assets converted into guaranteed lifetime income would result in twice as much spending compared to the money that's left in financial assets.

Converting financial assets into guaranteed lifetime income is a retiree's "license to spend," according to Blanchett and Finke. People can safely spend more, because they now have more income that's guaranteed for life. They've reduced both their longevity risk and their investment risk. They're also freed of mental and emotional factors that keep people from spending down their nest eggs. They don't see their retirement assets steadily declining even though they're spending more. In essence, they have replicated the paychecks that were received during the working years. For decades they were comfortable with the notion of spending most of their paychecks. They can continue that practice in retirement after some financial assets are converted to guaranteed lifetime income.[6]

It's easy to see how increasing guaranteed lifetime income enables a retiree to spend more without increasing risk. For retirement savings that are invested, retirees generally are advised to follow the "4 percent spending rule," also known as the "safe spending rate" or "safe withdrawal rate," as discussed in chapter 6—to avoid running out of money in less than thirty years, a retiree should spend no more than 4 percent of the investment assets each year, adjusted for inflation.

But the amount that can be withdrawn from a retirement portfolio using the 4 percent rule is much less than the income that would be received by depositing the same amount of money in an income annuity. The income annuity payment isn't adjusted for inflation over time, but the initial payment is significantly higher than a distribution using the 4 percent rule would be. Also, the income annuity is guaranteed to last more than thirty years. It's guaranteed to last for as long as the retiree lives. But distributions under the 4 percent rule aren't guaranteed at all and aren't even assured of lasting for thirty years under all scenarios. The retiree is told only that using historic investment data the portfolio has a high probability of lasting at least thirty years a very high percentage of the time.

The False Retirement Challenge

Many people are told that in retirement they must choose between two options, each with risks and rewards.

One option is to spend more in the early years of retirement. The reward is they are younger and healthier at that time, so they are more able to take advantage of spending opportunities and enjoy that period of retirement. The downside is that spending more in early retirement can increase long-term risks. If you spend too much in the early years of retirement, there may not be enough for the later years. That risk is increased if investment markets turn hostile to retirees or if later in life the individual retiree incurs unexpected expenses for medical care, long-term care, home repair, help for family members, or other unexpected expenses.

The other option is to spend less in the early years of retirement. That increases the amount of money available in case one or more of the long-term risks is realized. But it means accepting a lower standard of living in the early retirement years. And this option still doesn't guarantee that enough money will be available in the later years of retirement.

This retirement dilemma is a false one. Retirees don't have to choose between these two undesirable choices. Later in this book you will learn how to significantly reduce the potential for large surprise medical expenses (chapter 7) and long-term care expenses (chapter 8). In chapter 6, I explain how to establish a spending plan that adjusts with inflation and market fluctuations, greatly reducing the potential that your nest egg will be spent too rapidly during retirement.

But an additional strategy that avoids the false retirement choice is to increase your level of guaranteed lifetime income. This step gives you a higher floor of income that lasts for the rest of your life (or the joint lives of you and your spouse). You transfer many of the investment and longevity risks of retirement to an insurance company that is better equipped to deal with them. You achieve the main goal of retirement saving and investing, which is to convert your lifetime of accumulated savings into income or cash flow. As we have seen, the research shows that converting part of your retirement savings into guaranteed lifetime income makes your total nest egg last longer and lets you spend more during retirement. In other words, the amount of savings accumulated for retirement is only one factor influencing your spending and the longevity of your nest egg. The form in which you hold that savings, or the way in which your portfolio is positioned, is also important. For most people, the best results occur when part of their savings is repositioned from investments into guaranteed lifetime income.

It's important to re-emphasize that few people should convert all or most of their retirement savings into guaranteed lifetime income. You want savings available for large one-time spending needs, such as home repairs and family emergencies. You also want to invest for appreciation, to maintain the purchasing power of your cash flow in the face of inflation over the years. You may also want to leave a legacy to your loved ones or to charity.

I recommend that a retiree establish enough guaranteed lifetime income to pay for fixed or regular monthly spending. (Some advisors recommend that the guaranteed lifetime income pay for fixed and essential costs, but it is difficult to distinguish fixed, essential costs from regular spending that might not be essential but that is part of your standard of living.) That way, no matter what's happening in the markets or elsewhere, you know that enough money will be flowing in to pay for your basic spending. To follow this approach, you would estimate regular retirement spending and then determine how much guaranteed lifetime income must be added to Social Security benefits to equal that level of spending. The rest of your retirement portfolio can be invested to supplement your regular spending and to ensure its purchasing power is maintained. The rest of the nest egg will be available to tap for those periodic large expenses, such as home repairs, new vehicles, and more. You would establish a spending strategy for that part of your portfolio, as discussed in chapter 6.

As we saw earlier in this chapter, one study recommended that 25 percent to 50 percent of a retirement portfolio be positioned in guaranteed lifetime income instead of financial assets. Instead of recommending a particular allocation, it pointed out the data concluded that increasing the allocation to guaranteed lifetime income gradually increased the probability a portfolio would last for at least thirty years.

That research, by Wade Pfau, concluded that after a retiree establishes the appropriate asset allocation for the retirement portfolio, the bond or fixed income allocation of that portfolio should be shifted to guaranteed lifetime income. Pfau concluded that guaranteed lifetime income is better than bonds or other fixed income investments for a number of reasons. To follow this approach, you would first determine how much you want invested in stocks, how much in bonds, and how much other investments. Then reposition into guaranteed lifetime income the amount that would be invested in bonds or other fixed-income investments.[7]

The Blanchett and Finke research didn't establish a guideline for the amount to invest in guaranteed lifetime income. But it concluded that lifetime spending increases as money is shifted from financial assets into guaranteed lifetime income.[8]

Not everyone needs to reposition part of their retirement savings into additional guaranteed lifetime income. Someone who is wealthy and whose standard of living poses little or no risk of running out of money during retirement is likely to be comfortable remaining invested in retirement in much the same way he or she invested during the working years. Also, someone who already has an employer pension or other guaranteed lifetime payment in addition to Social Security might not need to increase guaranteed lifetime income.

Where to Find Guaranteed Lifetime Income

There are generally three potential sources of guaranteed lifetime income: employer pensions, Social Security, and private income contracts, or annuities. Not too many decades ago, most American retirees had at least two sources of guaranteed lifetime income: Social Security and an employer pension. They didn't worry about outliving their income, because a comfortable level of income was guaranteed for life, no matter how long they lived. But private sector employers gradually reduced and eliminated pensions. Now, most retirees have only Social Security as a source of guaranteed income. They depend on savings and investments for the rest of their retirement income.

Since most retirees today don't have employer pensions, and for those who do the details vary considerably among existing pension plans, I won't discuss employer pensions in this book. Social Security and income annuities are the key sources of guaranteed lifetime income for most retirees in the United States. They're discussed in detail in the following two chapters. Social Security is first, followed by income annuities.

CHAPTER 4

Don't Leave Money on the Table:
How to Make the Most of Social Security

M ost Americans have at least one source of guaranteed lifetime income: Social Security. For many, it is the only source of guaranteed lifetime income that is also indexed for inflation, which is an extremely valuable benefit. Many Americans are actually Social Security millionaires. The amount of money needed to purchase a private annuity with Social Security's benefits (if you could find one with true inflation indexing) would be more than $1 million for most people.

Unfortunately, only a minority of Americans take full advantage of their Social Security benefits. Many people leave tens of thousands of dollars (or more) on the table with their decisions about when to claim their Social Security benefits. In fact, almost all U.S. retirees claim Social Security benefits at a less than optimum time and short-change themselves by a collective $3.4 trillion in lifetime benefits.[1]

The key conclusion of a 2019 report by United Income was stunning: 96 percent of retirees began Social Security benefits at the wrong time for them. If these households had claimed their benefits at the optimal time, the average lifetime income per household would have been $111,000, or 9 percent, higher. Since that's the average shortfall, many households gave up even greater lifetime benefits.

Social Security is a major source of income for most retirees. About 86 percent of current retirees fund their retirement primarily with Social Security or a pension, according to a 2019 survey by Wells Fargo and the Harris Poll. Social Security and pensions will be the main retirement funding source for 60 percent of Baby Boomers, according to the survey.[2]

I won't hold you in suspense. The optimum decision for many individuals and households is to wait to claim retirement benefits. Most people do the opposite. Claiming benefits before full retirement age (FRA) reduces them 5/8 of a percent per month for the first thirty-six months they are claimed before full retirement age and 5/12 of a percent for each additional month. The result is that if you claim benefits at age 62, you receive only about 75 percent of your full-retirement-age benefits. Claiming a spousal benefit at 62 pays a 30 percent lower benefit than at full retirement age.

Additionally, each year you delay benefits past FRA, through age 70, your benefits increase 8 percent per year through what are known as delayed retirement credits. That means if you delay benefits until age seventy, you'll receive about 32 percent more than your benefit at full retirement age.

The exact amount depends on your year of birth because your FRA depends on when you were born. Those with FRAs after age sixty-six will lose more by claiming benefits at age sixty-two and gain a little less by waiting until age seventy to claim benefits.

Optimizing Social Security retirement benefits significantly reduces the three greatest risks of retirement.

- Maximizing Social Security benefits reduces what economists call longevity risk. No matter how long you live, you won't run out of money.
- Your risk of losing purchasing power to inflation also will be reduced. Social Security benefits are indexed for inflation each year.
- You'll depend less on the investment markets for retirement security. Social Security benefits are paid without regard to what's happening in the investment markets. In fact, maximizing guaranteed Social Security benefits can allow you to take more risk with the rest of your nest egg and possibly earn higher returns.

Consider the Solo Years

The main consideration for married couples is the period after one spouse passes away. As I explain in detail in chapter 13, a surviving spouse receives only one Social Security benefit. In most cases, the surviving spouse receives the higher payment of the two. There are some exceptions, but that's the basic rule that affects most surviving spouses.

While both spouses were alive, two Social Security checks were coming into the household. After one spouse passes away, one of those Social Security benefits ends. The surviving spouse must maintain the household on only the remaining benefit. If the higher-earning spouse claimed benefits early, that one check is going to be much less than it could have been.

It doesn't matter whether the surviving spouse is you or your mate. The survivor is likely going to regret the decisions to grab those Social Security benefits as soon as they were available and will wish that the survivor benefit check were a lot higher.

Special Rules for Spouses

There are a few special rules for married couples. Congress changed those rules in 2015, so if you're married you need to be especially careful not to base your decisions about Social Security decisions on a pre-2016 source.

A married person typically qualifies for more than one Social Security benefit. If the person worked in covered employment and acquired at least forty credits toward Social Security, he or she qualifies for retirement benefits based on that work history. A credit is a quarter of a year working in a job or self-employment that's covered by Social Security.[3] A married person also qualifies for spousal benefits. A spousal benefit is normally 50 percent of the other spouse's full retirement benefit. In other words, the spousal benefit is half of the benefit that the other spouse would be entitled to at full retirement age.

The Social Security Administration (SSA) deems a married person to have filed for all the benefits he or she qualifies for, and it pays whichever is the highest benefit. So, most people don't decide whether to claim their own retirement benefits or the spousal benefits; the SSA determines which benefits the applicant qualifies for and pays the higher one.

But there are a few exceptions to that rule. You don't qualify for spousal benefits until your spouse has claimed his or her retirement benefits. So if you want to claim Social Security benefits and your spouse hasn't filed to claim his or her retirement benefits, you can claim only your own retirement benefits. But later, when your spouse does claim retirement benefits, you can switch to spousal benefits if they're higher than your retirement benefits.

Another caveat is that the early retirement reduction for claiming benefits before FRA applies to spousal benefits as well. So if you qualify for spousal benefits but are younger than your FRA (not your spouse's FRA), you can receive reduced spousal benefits because you claimed them early. In that scenario you'll receive less than 50 percent of your spouse's FRB.

Another rule spouses should know is that only one spouse at a time can claim spousal benefits. One spouse has to claim his or her own retirement benefit to allow the other spouse to claim the spousal benefit.

When a person (except a surviving spouse—more on that below) applies to claim benefits, he or she is deemed to have applied for all benefits available. That is a feature of the 2015 Social Security reforms.

Though you may be eligible for two or more types of benefits and are deemed to have applied for every Social Security benefit you qualify for, you will be paid only one of those benefits at a time—the higher one. For example, a married person might qualify for both his or her own retirement benefit and a spousal benefit, but only the higher of the two benefits will be paid.

Special Rules for the Divorced

There's no such thing as "divorce benefits" in Social Security, but spousal benefits are often available to ex-spouses, and they're available on fairly liberal terms. Divorced spouses, in fact, sometimes have more options and flexibility than current spouses and widowed spouses.

A person can collect Social Security spousal benefits based on the earnings record of a former spouse under certain circumstances. The basic requirements:

- The marriage must have lasted at least ten years.
- The couple must have been divorced for at least two years, in most cases.

- The ex-spouse claiming benefits must still be unmarried, again in most cases.
- The ex-spouse on whose earnings history the benefits are based must be at least age sixty-two.

A person also might be able to claim survivor's benefits after an ex-spouse passes away, a possibility I explore later in this chapter.

As I said, some of the claiming rules for former spouses are more flexible than for married spouses. You may recall that when a couple is married, a spouse can't claim spousal benefits unless the other spouse has claimed and is receiving his or her retirement benefits. If the spouse drawing a retirement benefit suspends that benefit or withdraws the claim, the spousal benefits to the other spouse also will end. When a divorced spouse claims spousal benefits, however, it doesn't matter whether the worker whose earnings history is the basis of the claim has filed to claim benefits or when that worker plans to claim benefits. The ex-spouse can claim benefits based on the other ex-spouse's earnings history anyway.

In other words, a divorced person is independently entitled to claim benefits on the earnings history of his or her former spouse. The worker whose earnings history is the basis for the claim doesn't have to be consulted and isn't even informed by Social Security that the former spouse is taking the benefits. The spousal benefits drawn by an ex-spouse also don't affect the amount of the benefits paid to the worker or any current spouse of the worker.

It also doesn't matter whether the ex-spouse has remarried. Thus, three or more people can claim benefits based on the same earnings record: the worker with the earnings record can claim his or her own benefits, that worker's current spouse can file for spousal benefits based on that record, and in addition, the former spouse—or former spouses—of the worker can claim benefits on that record if they meet the eligibility rules.

In case you're worried, the primary worker's benefits aren't reduced when other people claim benefits based on his or her earnings history. A worker's retirement benefits are calculated based on his or her earnings history. The amount of those benefits doesn't change based on the number of spouses and ex-spouses who also claim benefits on that earnings history. (That, incidentally, is evidence that you don't own an account at Social Security with a sum of money in it.)

A divorced spouse's spousal benefits will be reduced, however, if she claims benefits before her own FRA. Just as retirement benefits are reduced when you claim them before FRA, spousal benefits are reduced before FRA—whether you claim them as a current spouse or former spouse.

The rate of reduction for spousal benefits, whether we're talking about spouses or ex-spouses, is even greater than for claiming your own retirement benefits before FRA. The spousal benefit is reduced by 8.33 percent annually for the first three years benefits are claimed early (that's 25/36 of a percent for each of the first 36 months) and 5 percent for each additional year (that's 5/12 of a percent for each additional month). A divorced spouse who claims the spousal benefit as early as possible, at age sixty-two, will have the benefit reduced by 30 percent, whereas a retiree who claims that early will receive a benefit reduced by only about 25 percent, as we have seen.

Delaying Social Security Makes Wealth Last Longer

Many people claim Social Security benefits before full retirement age because they have stopped working, and they believe the Social Security benefits are needed to replace some of the income they earned from working. They want to delay or minimize spending from their retirement savings for as long as possible, believing that will make their nest eggs last longer.

That seems logical, but that's not the best way to extend the life of a retirement nest egg. The counterintuitive action is likely to have better results: you're likely to have more money in the long run if you begin to spend your retirement savings in order to delay claiming Social Security benefits.

One study looked specifically at how the amount of Social Security benefits influenced a portfolio's longevity. The study, written by William Meyer and William Reichenstein published in the April 2012 *Financial Planning Journal*, examined the effects on portfolio longevity and spending when individuals claimed their Social Security retirement benefits at different ages. The study looked at how much a retiree could spend during his or her lifetime and how long a portfolio would last under the different Social Security claiming strategies.

The longer a retiree delays the start of Social Security benefits, the longer a portfolio will last, according to the study. If the Social Security–claiming date is delayed to age seventy, the portfolio would last ten years longer than if benefits were claimed at sixty-two. Claiming at ages later than sixty-two but earlier than seventy extends the longevity of the portfolio, but by shorter periods.[4]

This finding seems counterintuitive to many people. The study assumes that a person stops earning income from employment at age sixty-two, regardless of when Social Security benefits begin. Thus the retiree's investment portfolio is used to fund living expenses during the years before Social Security benefits begin, and it steadily declines during those years. Most people assume that beginning to spend the retirement nest egg so early will create solvency problems later in retirement. So they want to take Social Security as early possible and delay drawing down their portfolios.

Yet once Social Security benefits begin, the benefits replace the funds you had been taking out of your portfolio to pay expenses. Less money now needs to be withdrawn from your investments going forward. So the value of your portfolio value will either stabilize or at least decline much more slowly than it was declining before you began receiving your Social Security benefits. At this point the late-claimer's portfolio can begin to "catch up" with the portfolio of the early-claimer. The study demonstrates that the portfolios of the late-claimers and early-claimers have about the same values after about seventeen years, or at about age seventy-nine for someone who retired at sixty-two. That's the crossover date when there's no difference in the results despite the different Social Security–claiming decisions.

But the results are very different after that. After the crossover date, the portfolios of the late-claimers decline much more slowly than the portfolios of those who claimed early. An important assumption of this study is that the people who claim benefits after age sixty-two draw all their income from the portfolios in the initial years, but once Social Security benefits begin the amount withdrawn from the portfolios each year declines by an amount equal to the Social Security benefits. In other words, the Social Security benefits aren't used to increase spending but are used to reduce the amount of annual withdrawals from the portfolios.

The Social Security–claiming decision is less important to portfolio longevity the more wealth a person has. Higher wealth usually means the person had a higher lifetime income, and that means that less of the person's employment income is replaced by Social Security than is the case for a lower-earning person. Also, a higher portfolio value means that, at any level of Social Security benefits, the portfolio provides a much higher percentage of the annual income than Social Security does.

Someone with a portfolio of $250,000 would see the portfolio last at least four years longer as a result of claiming Social Security at age sixty-four instead of sixty-two. That's four extra years of life for the portfolio solely from waiting two years to begin Social Security benefits. That effect was not as large for a retiree with more assets. Someone with a portfolio of $1 million or more would see the portfolio's longevity increase by only one year if he claimed Social Security at sixty-four instead of sixty-two.

Or, the study found, instead of having the portfolio last longer, the retiree can increase the amount of real (adjusted for inflation) spending during retirement. Meyer and Reichenstein concluded that a retiree who wanted to ensure the portfolio lasts at least thirty years could spend $36,150 in real dollars annually if he claimed his Social Security at sixty-two. Delaying benefits to seventy allows annual real spending to increase to $39,750 each year for thirty years. That's a $3,600 (or about 10 percent) increase in annual spending made possible by waiting a few years to claim Social Security benefits.

Many people don't understand the power of delaying Social Security benefits. The longer you live, the more beneficial and powerful delaying benefits is. The benefit amount increases each month that you wait to claim benefits. The amount of the increase varies during the waiting period. The range of the annual benefit increases from delaying between ages sixty-two and seventy varies from 6.34 percent to 8.34 percent. From full retirement age to seventy, benefits increase by 8 percent annually.

These increases are real. That is, they are adjusted for inflation. You receive a nominal increase in benefits for the delay, and your benefits are also adjusted annually for inflation, and those increases compound over time.

Of course, the longer you live, the more significant the gains from delaying benefits. Meyer and Reichenstein calculate that if someone lives to age ninety-two, the monthly Social Security benefit is about 29 percent higher for a person who waited until age seventy to begin benefits than if he or she had initiated benefits at age sixty-two. That's about a 30 percent higher monthly income every month for the rest of the person's life.[5]

Principles for Single Individuals

I recommend that single individuals make Social Security–claiming decisions with two goals in mind. The first goal is to maximize lifetime cumulative benefits. The second is to reduce "longevity risk"— that is, the risk of running out of money and having to reduce your standard of living if you live well beyond life expectancy.

For most single persons, each of these goals is achieved by waiting to claim Social Security retirement benefits.

One way to consider whether or not it makes sense to delay benefits is to estimate the crossover or breakeven point. That's the age at which waiting to claim benefits begins to maximize the total lifetime benefit. If you die before reaching that age, you'll have received lower lifetime benefits than if you had claimed earlier. The crossover or breakeven point for single individuals claiming benefits is between ages seventy-eight and eighty, depending on the year of birth and when their FRA is. The longer you delay claiming Social Security, the greater the lifetime benefits you'll be paid once you live beyond the crossover point. The added lifetime benefits from delaying benefits compound, so that the longer you live after the crossover point the greater the cumulative benefit is, compared to claiming early. If someone with a Full Retirement Benefit (FRB) of $2,000 claims benefits at seventy instead of sixty-two and then lives into his or her nineties, that person's lifetime benefits will be $150,000 more than if he or she had claimed benefits at age sixty-two.

Claiming benefits later also reduces longevity risk. That is, you make it less likely that you will outlive your money. The greater your monthly Social Security benefit, the less money you need to spend from your retirement nest egg and any other resources you have. Delaying benefits also means that your monthly income is much higher in the later years. If your nest egg has been reduced and other sources of income have lost purchasing power because of inflation, the additional monthly income from a higher Social Security benefit will be very welcome.

High income in your oldest years is the way to reduce longevity risk. But claiming Social Security benefits early reduces your monthly income in those additional years, whereas delaying your claim of Social Security benefits increases that income and provides more security in later years.

Principles for Married Couples

There are special considerations for married couples. The best strategy for spouses can be different from the best strategy for singles. It's important, as I have pointed out, for married couples to coordinate their Social Security–claiming decisions. And yet often each spouse makes a claiming decision based on his or her goals, assumptions, and outlook, independent of the other spouse.

The basic goals for a married couple are the same as for a single individual. You want to maximize lifetime cumulative benefits received and minimize longevity risk. But the actions that spouses need to take in order to accomplish those goals can be a little different from the right decisions for single people.

In most married couples, one spouse has higher lifetime earnings and a higher FRB than the other. Sometimes the gap between the two is substantial; sometimes the gap isn't as large. The difference can change the optimum claiming decisions for the spouses.

The most important consideration for married couples is what I call the solo years—the time after one spouse has passed away and the other still is living. When one spouse passes, one Social Security benefit ends. The surviving spouse receives only the higher of the two benefits, as a general rule.

To maximize the monthly benefit to the surviving spouse, regardless of which spouse it is, the spouse with the higher lifetime earnings and higher FRB needs to delay claiming benefits as long as possible, ideally to age seventy.

The best decision for the lower-earning spouse isn't as clear cut. The ideal decision can depend on the age difference and the difference between the spouses' earnings. Often, the right decision for the couple is for the lower-earning spouse to claim Social Security benefits early, even as early as age sixty-two, while the higher-earning spouse delays benefits.

Because the higher-earning spouse is claiming benefits late and ensuring the highest monthly benefit for the surviving spouse, the goal of reducing longevity risk is achieved. The couple also is a long way toward maximizing lifetime benefits. Thus it can make sense for lower-earning spouse to claim benefits early so that benefits begin flowing into the household.

When the lower-earning spouse claims benefits early, the couple can spend less from their nest egg without reducing their standard of living. This can make the nest egg last longer and reduce longevity risk.

There's another trick for married couples. Once the higher-earning spouse claims retirement benefits, the other spouse may receive a bump in monthly benefits. That's because a spouse receives the higher of his or her own retirement benefit or the spousal benefit. But the spousal benefit can't be received until the other spouse claims his or her benefits. So if the lower-earning spouse claims retirement benefits early while the higher-earning spouse waits, the lower-earning spouse can't receive the spousal benefits at first.

Once the higher-earning spouse claims retirement benefits, the lower-earning spouse can begin receiving the spousal benefit—one half of the spouse's retirement benefit—if it is higher than his or her retirement benefit. When there's a meaningful gap between the life-time earnings of the two spouses, one-half of the higher-earning spouse's FRB will be higher than the lower-earning spouse's benefit. The couple receives a boost in monthly income when the lower-earning spouse switches from his or her retirement benefit to the spousal benefit of one-half the other spouse's FRB. One caveat: that spousal benefit will be reduced to less than half the other spouse's FRB if the lower-earning spouse first claimed retirement benefits before his or her FRA before later switching to spousal benefits. How much the spousal benefit will be reduced will depend on how long before FRA the spouse first claimed his or her retirement benefits, as discussed earlier in this chapter.

The bottom line for married couples is that the higher-earning spouse should delay retirement benefits as long as possible. The ideal time for the lower-earning spouse to take benefits depends on the difference between the ages and earnings of the two spouses. The best way to make the decision is to use the Social Security calculators I discuss below.

How to Decide

Those are the basic scenarios—and the general principles for maximizing benefits and achieving other important retirement goals. As I said, everyone's situation is different. The general rules might not be the best solutions for you. I'm sure you have realized that there are a lot of elements to the Social Security claiming decision, and it shouldn't be a snap decision.

That's why I recommend that you not make a decision based on intuition or by simply reviewing the rules. The best approach is to crunch the numbers and look at what the lifetime benefits would be under the different scenarios.

Fortunately, you don't have to do the calculations by hand—a process that will take quite a lot of time if you want to see the results under a range of different assumptions about life spans and claiming dates. There are very good and low-cost tools available to you. These are calculators that will use your actual earnings and personal data to show the benefits you would receive under different claiming scenarios. Then you can compare the annual and lifetime benefits under the different scenarios.

The time and money you spend on the calculators will be worthwhile. As we have seen from the United Income study, the optimum claiming decision will increase lifetime benefits by an average of more than $100,000. For many people, depending on their longevity and lifetime income, the difference between a poor claiming decision and the optimum decision will be $200,000 or more.

The first step is to go to the Social Security Agency web site at www.socialsecurity.gov, open a "*my* Social Security" account, and use the calculator there. And then you should also use at least one of the commercially available benefits calculators such as Maximize My Social Security (www.maximizemysocialsecurity.com) or Social Security Solutions (www.socialsecuritysolutions.com). I have worked with both programs and found them to be useful, but I have no financial relationship with either of them or the experts who created them. You may also want to work with. a retirement planning professional.

You Might Need to Know More

This chapter has discussed the key facts you need to know about claiming Social Security benefits, but it can't cover everything you might want or need to know about this complicated program.

For example, you might need to know how Social Security benefits are taxed. That's discussed in chapter 10. You also might need to know the special rules apply to surviving spouses. Those are discussed in chapter 13, along with other issues that may arise in what I call the Solo Years.

There are other issues there isn't room to discuss in this book. You might want to know the details of how Social Security retirement benefits are calculated: continuing to work can affect the amount of your benefits, whether you have claimed benefits or not. There are also some interactions between Social Security and Medicare benefits you might want to know. In some situations, you can change a Social Security decision even after benefits have been claimed. You might be able to take a lump sum of Social Security benefits. These and other issues related to Social Security are discussed in my book, *Where's My Money? Secrets to Getting the Most out of Your Social Security*, published by Regnery Capital in 2021.

CHAPTER 5

How to Create More Guaranteed Lifetime Income

You've seen that guaranteed lifetime income can make a retirement portfolio last longer, in many cases years longer. It enables retirees to spend more money with lower risk and stress. Many economists recommend lifetime guaranteed income as the bedrock of retirement finance. We explored these points in detail in chapter 3. Yet only a small percentage of retirees shift part of their retirement funds into guaranteed lifetime income, and guaranteed lifetime income vehicles have a bad reputation in a lot of the financial media.

In this chapter I explore the details of how to reposition part of your retirement nest egg as guaranteed lifetime income. You do this primarily by using assets to purchase annuities. I lay out the different types of annuities to consider for guaranteed lifetime income (known generally as income annuities), explore why more people don't shift part of their portfolios into income annuities, and review strategies to maximize the benefits of income annuities.

Let's start by defining what we're talking about.

There are many types of annuities, and a major problem is that people often use the word "annuities" generically instead of acknowledging the different types of annuities and defining which kind they're referring to. Many annuity critics complain of high fees, misleading sales presentations, and other problems. Those disadvantages can apply to certain types of annuities, though in recent years regulators and the insurance industry have done a lot to reduce the misleading sales tactics. (For examples of misleading sales tactics, see the section titled "Secrets of Annuity U. Exposed" in my book *The New Rules of Retirement*, originally published by Wiley in 2004 and revised in 2016.) In this chapter I'm discussing only income annuities.

Types of Income Annuities

Annuities that pay guaranteed lifetime income are very simple. They don't have complex or additional fees. All the costs are built into the annuity. The insurer determines its expenses and figures its profit before stating how much your guaranteed income will be. The income you're promised will be paid without deductions for additional fees or expenses.

Single premium immediate annuities (SPIAs), also known as immediate annuities, are the granddaddy of all annuities. They date back many hundreds of years and are direct descendants of the original annuity, the Roman tontine. In a SPIA, you sign a contract and deposit a lump sum with an insurer. In return the insurer begins paying you a fixed amount. The payments begin within one year after your deposit is made and often the following month, which is why they're called immediate annuities. The annuity owner determines when the payments begin. Most insurers let you choose whether the payments will be made monthly, quarterly, or annually. You're told before signing the contract how much each payment will be, and the payment amount is stated specifically in the contract. The payments continue for as long as you're alive. We'll discuss variations and options regarding the SPIA later in this chapter, but that's the prototype.

Deferred income annuity (DIAs), also known as longevity annuities, are very similar. The difference is that after you sign the contract and deposit the lump sum, the insurer promises to begin payments to you at some point in the future. You decide when signing the contract when the payments will begin, and the payments can begin as early as two years after the deposit is made and as late as age eighty-five. Before you make the deposit, the insurer tells you the amount the payments will be. As with the SPIA, once the payments begin they continue for as long as you're alive. There are also some variations to the basic DIA from which you can select.

The qualified longevity annuity contract (QLAC) is a DIA designed specifically to be owned by IRAs. The amount invested in the QLAC isn't counted when determining required minimum distributions from the IRA, so the QLAC is useful for someone who wants to delay part of their required minimum distributions. See chapter 9 for more details about IRAs and required minimum distributions.

All these kinds of annuities are contracts with guarantees. Unlike with other kinds of investments, including some other types of annuities, uncertainties and probabilities aren't part of the equation. You have a contract with the insurer in which the insurer guarantees to make payments in the stated amount for the period stated in the contract. The terms don't fluctuate with interest rates, the stock market, taxes, or any other factor. The main risk is the financial solvency of the insurer.

Though many people think of annuities as a form of investment and contrast them with investment alternatives, income annuities aren't investments. They are contracts. They're perhaps best described as longevity insurance. You're being insured against the possibility of living a long life. You will receive the income payments as long as you're alive, even if you live to be 120 or beyond. The payments may lose purchasing power to inflation, but they'll continue to be made. You won't outlive your money as long as you put some of it in an income annuity.

You're also insuring against adverse trends in the investment markets. When stock markets head south, you won't see a decline in the portion of your net worth that has been deposited in an income annuity, and your cash flow from the annuity won't change. When interest rates decline, the income coming into your household from the annuity doesn't fall. The same amount of money continues to flow to you regardless of what's happening in the markets and economy.

You can think of an income annuity as a personal pension or private pension. The annuity replaces the employer pension that previous generations of retirees relied on. A portion of your retirement savings is used to purchase a guaranteed stream of income that gives you the security and certainty of an employer pension.

There are a few other variations of annuities that can generate guaranteed lifetime income. These generally are indexed annuities or variable annuities with income riders. I'm not going to discuss those variations in detail. (Later in this chapter I do explain annuities with a cost-of-living adjustment (COLA) or growth rider.) With indexed and variable annuities, we venture outside the realm of contracts and guarantees and begin to enter the world of probabilities and possibilities. The amount of income you receive from those annuities will depend on market fluctuations and the detailed terms of the contract. If you're interested in considering them, you should work with an insurance agent or financial planner who knows the different choices available in the market, works with a number of different insurers, and isn't biased toward one product or insurer. The advisor should be concerned first with your goals and risk profile and then seek to find the alternative that's the best fit for you.

Frequently Asked Questions about Income Annuities

We could wrap up the discussion of income annuities here, because they are very simple and straightforward. But there are some questions that are frequently asked about them, and in addition it is worth knowing about some options that are available to modify the basic income annuity. You can choose a particular annuity with contract terms that fit your goals or preferences. Let's review those issues.

When do income payments begin? In a SPIA, the income payments begin soon after the deposit is made with the insurer and the contract is executed. The first payment can be made as soon as one month later and must be deferred no more than twelve months after the contract is signed. With a DIA, or longevity annuity, the first payment is made no earlier than two years after the contract is completed and no later than age eighty-five. With either type of annuity, the annuity owner sets the date of the first payment when executing the contract.

How long will I receive income payments? The person buying the annuity decides the length of the payment period from among several options offered by the insurer.

In the standard income annuity, known as a single life annuity, payments are made for the life of the annuity owner. As long as the annuity owner is alive, the income will arrive as scheduled.

With a joint-life annuity, a married person or couple buying an annuity can elect to have payments made as long as either spouse is living. The payments will end only after both spouses have passed away. There's a cost to a joint-life annuity: income payments will be less than those of a single life annuity, because a couple's joint life expectancy is longer than an individual's.

There are variations of the joint-life annuity. Under the joint-life-and-100-percent-survivor annuity, the income payments won't change as long as at least one spouse is living. You also could select a joint life with less than a 100-percent-survivor option. For example, under a joint-and-50-percent-survivor option, after one spouse passes away the surviving spouse receives 50 percent of the income payment that was made while both spouses were alive. When the survivor option is less than 100 percent, the payment made while both spouses are alive will be higher than under the 100-percent-survivor option.

So, I lose and the insurance company wins if I die before life expectancy? There are other income options in addition to the single life and joint life annuities. Many insurers offer an option known generically as return of premium. Details vary among insurers, but electing a return-of-premium rider means that if you die before average life expectancy, the insurer will pay all or a percentage of your initial deposit to beneficiaries you name or to your estate. Electing this option will reduce the income payments made during your life compared to payments from either a single life or a joint life annuity.

Another option is the life-and-period-of-years, also known as the life-and-term-certain annuity, which makes income payments to you or a beneficiary for the longer of either your life or a period of years that you select. Suppose, for example, that you elect that the payments will continue for life or fifteen years. The payments will be made to you for as long as you live if you live more than another fifteen years. But if you live less than another fifteen years, the payments will be made to you for the rest of your life and then to a beneficiary you named, until payments have been made for a total of fifteen years. After 15 years have passed since your first income payment was received, payments to the beneficiary will end.

What about inflation? In the standard annuity, the amount of each payment is fixed for life. You know exactly how much money will be paid to you each month (or other period) for the rest of your life. The disadvantage of a fixed-income payment is that the purchasing power of that income will be reduced over time by inflation. There are several ways to deal with that.

Most income annuities now offer some kind of cost-of-living adjustment (COLA) or growth rider, under which the income payment will increase over time. The most common riders allow you to select the adjustment amount, usually 2 percent, 3 percent, or 5 percent. The income payment is increased by that percentage each year. Some annuities have different variations or formulas.

But as with other adjustments to the basic income annuity, selecting this option will reduce the initial payment you receive. In general, selecting a COLA or similar rider will decrease your initial income payment by 20 percent or more from the standard life annuity payment. The amount of the reduction varies based on your age, the insurer, and the rider you select.

As I write, no annuity issued in the United States offers a true inflation-adjustment rider under which the income payments would be increased each year based on the full change in the Consumer Price Index or some other inflation benchmark. Insurers believe that they can't anticipate future inflation well enough to be able to determine the appropriate initial income payment under such a provision.

There are other ways to deal with inflation, though. You should own assets other than annuities, and these should be invested for growth so that the gains can be used to supplement the annuity income to maintain your purchasing power. You also could save some of the annuity income each year so that it will be available to restore purchasing power in the future.

<u>What or who guarantees my annuity income?</u> The main guarantor of the income is the insurer issuing the annuity. Most insurers in the U.S. have been around for a hundred years or longer and prospered

through many changes in the markets and the economy. They invest conservatively. They also employ actuaries who process the data and determine how much they can safely pay to annuitants.

An additional protection is that insurers are closely regulated by the states. The regulations require insurers to maintain a minimum amount of capital and liquid assets to meet their contractual obligations. The types of investments an insurer can make are also restricted by regulations and monitored by the regulators.

But they're allowed to take risks within the regulatory guidelines, and not all insurers are the same. You should examine the safety ratings of any insurer you are considering purchasing an annuity from. Safety ratings are issued by several different organizations. An insurer and the agent or broker you're working with should volunteer to provide the safety ratings to you or at least provide them after being asked. In recent years, some insurers have been acquired by hedge funds or private equity firms. These investors believe the insurers would become more profitable by investing their reserves more aggressively. Some observers believe at least some of these insurers are taking more risk than insurers should and thus increasing the risk of default. Know who owns any insurer when you might purchase an annuity and monitor the ownership after buying an annuity.

State regulators as well as the larger insurers work to prevent defaults on insurance products. When an insurer has liquidity or solvency issues, regulators and other insurers often work together to arrange for one or more other insurers to take over the obligations and assets of the troubled insurer.

In addition, most states have guaranty funds that can be used to fulfill the obligations of insurers based in the state. Insurers generally pay into the guaranty funds based on the number of annuities and insurance they sell in a state. But the guaranty funds limit how much they'll pay on any individual annuity or life insurance contract, and the limits vary from state to state. Only the resources in the funds support the guarantees. The funds and guarantees aren't backed by the state or federal government.

When interest rates are low should I wait before buying an annuity? The amount of income you receive from an annuity does have some relationship with market interest rates, because the insurer assumes it will earn an investment return on your deposit. But interest rates shouldn't be a prime factor in deciding when or whether to buy an income annuity. The insurer doesn't consider short-term changes in interest rates, because it's making long-term investments with your deposit. Also, life expectancy is the main factor used to determine the annuity income payments. Interest rates are a secondary factor.

Another consideration is that if you don't buy the annuity now, you have to do something with the money. You'll probably invest it for safety so the principal will be intact in a few years when you plan to buy the annuity. You won't earn much on that money, because interest rates are low. The insurer probably assumes a higher long-term return on its portfolio than you'll receive in safe investments. So you may lose money by waiting for interest rates to change before buying an annuity.

If the current level of interest rates concerns you, consider buying income annuities gradually over several years in what is known as an annuity ladder.

What is my rate of return on an income annuity? The short answer is you won't know the rate of return on an income annuity until the day you pass away. The rate of return is going to depend on how much the insurer pays you over the years and how long it makes payments.

But you aren't buying an income annuity primarily as an investment to earn a rate of return. An income annuity is acquired to generate guaranteed lifetime income. The real goal is to transfer key risks away from you to the insurer. You want the insurer to assume the risk of market fluctuations and the risk that you'll live a long life.

You do want to ensure you receive a competitive amount of income on the money you deposit with the insurer. Shortly I'll explain how to do that. But the focus of an income annuity should be on the guarantees and certainty you're receiving. The amount of income you receive shouldn't be compared to what you might receive from investing in the stock market or some other vehicle. Those investments don't have guarantees; they carry potential risks along with their potential returns.

If I won't need the guaranteed lifetime income for a few years, should I buy a SPIA when I want income to begin or should I buy a DIA a few years before? Insurance companies employ a lot of actuaries and other professionals to determine how much income you'll receive after buying an annuity. It doesn't matter to them whether you buy a SPIA or a DIA. They simply adjust the amount of income you'll be paid based on the differences in the annuities. You're unlikely to be able to outsmart the insurers or game the system.

Also, as mentioned above, if you plan to buy a SPIA in a few years you'll probably invest the money conservatively in the meantime and earn a low rate of return. The insurer probably would earn more with the money, so and you'll likely end up with more money by buying a DIA now instead of a SPIA later.

Another factor to consider is what the insurers call mortality credits. When the insurer sells a DIA this year to many people, it knows some percentage of them will pass away before receiving any income or after receiving only a small number of income payments. The insurer factors that into its calculations and assumes the deposits those individuals made will remain with the insurer. Those are mortality credits that are used to promise higher payouts than otherwise would be available to the remaining annuity owners.

<u>What if I suddenly need more money for an emergency?</u> A standard income annuity makes the fixed payments on the schedule you selected. When an unplanned large expense arises, you need additional savings or other sources of funds to pay the expense. That's one reason why it's not recommended to put all or most of your retirement funds into income annuities.

But many annuities now allow you to select a rider that allows you to periodically request money exceeding the regular income payments. Some income annuities allow you to withdraw as much as 10 percent of your initial deposit each year in addition to the regular income payments.

If you select this option, your guaranteed income payments are likely to be less than under the standard annuity. Also, after you request a return of some of your principal, the insurer may recalculate the future guaranteed income payments based on the new level of principal you have deposited in the annuity.

<u>How much of my portfolio should I put in income annuities?</u> There's no rule of thumb or guideline on the amount of a retirement portfolio that should be repositioned as income annuities. The studies I discussed earlier and in Chapter 3 found that most nest eggs last longer when 25 percent of the capital is switched to annuities and even longer when you shift 50 percent to annuities.

Another way to decide the issue is to consider how much guaranteed lifetime income you want each month. I frequently recommend that guaranteed lifetime income cover the basic amount you plan to spend each month. But the decision depends on a few factors, including the level of investment returns you estimate, the level of risk you want to take in retirement, and how the value of your investment assets compares to the level of expenses you plan in retirement.

For most people, between 25 percent and 50 percent of the retirement nest egg is the appropriate amount to reposition as guaranteed lifetime income. The exact amount within that range is a personal question. If you're having trouble balancing the factors and deciding, consider working with a financial planner.

What are the income tax consequences of an annuity? The federal income taxes imposed on annuity income depend on how you purchase the annuity.

You're allowed to use funds in an IRA or other qualified retirement plan to purchase an annuity. The insurer can make the income payments to the IRA, which in turn distributes them to you. Or the insurer can make the payments directly to you. In either case, the payments are taxed the same as other retirement plan distributions. If all your money in the retirement plan is pre-tax (which is the usual case), the entirety of the income payments will be taxed as ordinary income when they are made.

You can also purchase an annuity with money that's already been taxed, such as money in a brokerage or savings account. In that case, each income payment you receive is treated partly as a tax-free return of your principal and partly as ordinary income. For most people, a large portion of the annuity income will be tax free for years.

Payments from annuities owned outside of retirement accounts are taxed under what the IRS calls the General Rule. This is explained in IRS Publication 939, which is available free on the IRS web site. Most insurers also provide guides on how to determine the income taxes on annuity payments.

How to Maximize Guaranteed Lifetime Income

During the thirty-plus years I've been producing my Retirement Watch newsletter, I regularly did the same experiment periodically for years with the same results. The experiment showed how to increase guaranteed lifetime annuity income by about 20 percent. That's 20 percent more income each month for life. I don't need to do the experiment any longer, because the annuity payment data is widely available online. Remarkably, the facts are still the same.

In the experiment, I would develop a profile of a hypothetical SPIA buyer and give the profile to one or two insurance brokers. The brokers would contact all the insurance companies with high financial safety ratings and get quotes of the amount of annual income the hypothetical individual would be paid if he made a $100,000 deposit for a SPIA. I did this exercise every two or three years and had the same result each time: The highest and lowest payouts from the insurers differed by about 20 percent. If we asked for quotes from insurers with less than the highest financial safety ratings, the variation in income would be even greater.

The point is that guaranteed lifetime income can be increased simply by shopping around. Don't be satisfied with a quote from only one insurer or broker. Sample all or most of the market and watch your lifetime income increase.

Even with annuity comparison shopping widely available on the internet, this price disparity still exists—partly because insurers know people don't like to shop around for insurance. Also, insurance companies have different expense levels and profit targets. They use different assumptions about inflation, investment returns, and life expectancy. Some insurers offer to pay more because they're trying to increase market share. Insurers with less than the top safety ratings often need to pay more to compensate people for taking the additional risk, though in most cases the risk of loss is still quite low.

The internet offers many easy ways to shop for annuities. The most comprehensive probably is through the services of Stan Haithcock, also known as Stan the Annuity Man. Go to www.stantheannuityman.com and click on the "Calculators" tab. Enter some basic information in the online calculators for different types of annuities, and you'll quickly receive several quotes from highly rated insurers.

CHAPTER 6

The Spending Plan:
Why It's Critical, and How Most Retirement Plans Get It Wrong

I t's easy to find advice about how to save and invest for retirement, or what's known as the accumulation phase of retirement planning. But the ultimate goal isn't simply to accumulate money, whether you're targeting a specific sum or trying to accrue as much as possible within your constraints. The ultimate goal is to convert that savings into income or cash flow that will fund your desired standard of retirement living and last for the rest of your life, no matter how long that might be. In effect, you want to replace the paycheck that you received during the working years with a steady, reliable paycheck from your portfolio and savings. Financial planners and economists call this the "decumulation" or "spending phase" of retirement planning.

It's important to have a plan or process to convert your retirement nest egg into steady cash flow. The key is to determine the maximum amount you can withdraw each year so there's a very low risk of running out of money later in retirement. Those who "wing it," or don't have a thought-out process, are the ones who worry regularly about how long their money will last and are most at risk of running out of money.

Creating a retirement spending plan is an important step regardless of where you are in retirement. Even someone who has been retired for years should develop a spending plan for the rest of retirement. Planning reduces surprises, increases confidence, and is likely to increase your financial security and independence.

Developing a decumulation plan requires two steps. The first step, discussed in previous chapters, is to determine how much guaranteed lifetime income you'll receive from Social Security and any pension, and how much of your savings to reposition as guaranteed lifetime income. This chapter will focus on the second step: to establish a plan for spending the rest of the retirement nest egg. The plan sets the maximum amount you can distribute from your portfolio each year to supplement your guaranteed lifetime income without taking the risk you'll deplete the portfolio during your lifetime.

Your strategy needs to take into account how people spend money in real life, and it needs to be adjustable for changes in the markets and inflation. A good spending strategy also adapts to the wealth, desired lifestyle, and risk tolerance of the retiree. The strategy should be flexible, adapting to changes in inflation, the investment markets, and the retiree's circumstances.

How Retirees Spend Money

The financial services industry and academic world didn't do much research into developing a spending plan until fairly recently. As a result, many retirees don't have formal spending plans, and most of the recommended spending plans don't accurately reflect how people actually spend their money in retirement.

The U.S. Department of Labor (DOL) regularly surveys households on how they spend their money at different ages. The results have been consistent over decades.[1] The spending studies find that most people spend the same amount as during their final working years, or even increase their spending, during the first five to ten years after retiring. Spending then begins to decline as people enter their early to mid-seventies.

That's logical. Most people are fairly healthy and active when they retire. They also have a range of activities they want to pursue with their added leisure time. But after a while they've done a lot of the activities and fall into more of a routine. In addition, most people naturally slow down as they age.

The decline in spending continues for the rest of life for most people. In fact, spending declines after the first ten years of retirement even after adjusting for inflation—in other words, there's a real decline in spending. The slide in spending is gradual, a decrease of about 2 to 3 percent annually. Some people increase spending on medical care or long-term care in the later years. But Medicare and other insurance can cover most of that spending, and those who pay the expenses out of pocket often reduce other spending, resulting in a net decrease in spending. So, an increase in real spending in the later years of retirement isn't a given, though that's what's assumed under the widely recommended spending plans.

Creating the Retirement Paycheck

Regardless of your age, you need to develop a method for turning your investment wealth into income and cash flow that lasts for the rest of your life. Even those already retired should develop a spending plan for the rest of their retirements.

A good strategy will begin with assumptions about the future based on research, but it also should allow for adjustments in response to changes in the markets and inflation. I recommend that the method for making changes be systematic, so that most changes are made automatically as asset values, inflation, and other factors change. I don't think you want to change the structure of your spending plan from year to year based on the latest headlines or expectations for the future. But no strategy should be completely hands-off or automatic. On a regular basis, re-evaluate how your plan is working and consider if it should be modified.

First, define your key issues and goals. No spending plan is right for everyone. I recommend not using simple rules of thumb, such as assuming you'll spend 80 percent of pre-retirement income in retirement or distributing a fixed percentage of your nest egg the first year and distributing that amount plus the change in the Consumer Price Index each year thereafter (this is known as the "4 percent rule"). Instead, follow the guidelines in this chapter to develop an individual spending plan that works for you. Some of you may want to use different spending plans for different periods of retirement, adjusting as your resources, risk profile, or other priorities change.

Estimate the cost of your desired standard of living. The starting point of any retirement plan and especially the spending plan is a determination of the lifestyle you anticipate in retirement and an estimate of how much that could cost each year. As best you can, imagine the lifestyle you want, and consider each likely item of spending during a year and estimate how much you'll spend in the first year of retirement. If you're already retired, do an analysis of the cost of your current lifestyle.

Make a list of all the items you're likely to spend money on during a year. Don't forget large periodic expenses such as purchasing a new car and home repairs and maintenance. A portion of these expenses should be given an entry in monthly or annual spending estimates.

A detailed review of how much you're likely to spend in the first year of retirement is an educational and worthwhile exercise for many people. Some people learn that they're able to enjoy the lifestyle they want, while others learn they need to make some adjustments in their spending or income.

Some people approach the spending plan from the other direction. They first estimate how much cash flow they're likely to be able to safely spend each year in retirement. Then they adjust their spending plan and lifestyle to match the cash inflows. If you take that approach, you still need to develop a full estimate of your expected spending each month and year in retirement. Otherwise, you won't know what standard of living can be supported by the income.

Is a legacy important to you? Some people want to leave money for loved ones or charity. Others are content to leave a legacy if that's how things work out, but they don't want to factor that into their spending plans. If leaving a legacy is an important goal for you, consider segregating that amount from the rest of your nest egg so it isn't included in your spending and income plans. If things go awry, you can always change your plan and use some or all of the legacy fund to help pay your retirement expenses. An alternative to segregating a legacy fund is to use a portion of your resources to buy a permanent life insurance policy (in contrast to a term) that's payable to whomever you want to receive the legacy, whether it is your heirs or a charity. The policy will have a cash value account that you can draw from if money becomes tight.

Estimate your life expectancy. A spending plan should be very different for someone who might live to ninety or beyond than for someone who has good reasons to expect to live only to average life expectancy or less. Developing a reasonable life expectancy estimate is an important element of your spending and income plans. At the end of this chapter, I discuss in more detail how to estimate your life expectancy.

Make investment and inflation assumptions. No one can predict the markets or economy well, but you need to make assumptions about future investment returns to determine whether your spending plan is realistic. Some people approach retirement with the idea that stocks are likely to deliver annual returns of 15 percent or more in the long term. That's consistent with stock index returns of recent years. As of April 2022, the S&P 500 has had annualized returns of 16.63 percent over three years, 15.50 percent over five years, and 14.47 percent over ten years.

But those returns are well above the long-term average. As I discussed in chapter 1, there are good reasons to expect that investment returns in coming years will be lower than the returns of the last 10 or 15 years. The safe approach is to assume future returns will be less than the long-term average or at least much lower than those of the last 15 years.

Many financial advisors believe that the most dangerous time period for a person's finances is the decade including the five years just before retirement and the first five years after retirement. A strong bear market during this period would knock the retirement plan well off track. Negative investment returns would cause a retiree to spend part of the nest egg principal early in retirement and reduce the amount of the nest egg that would benefit from any ensuing market recovery. Economists often refer to this possibility as sequence-of-returns risk, and I discuss it in more detail in chapters 2 and 14. That's why the spending strategy you develop should adjust to changes in the markets.

Inflation is an important consideration, and one of the most overlooked factors in retirement planning. I believe many people don't properly account for inflation when planning for retirement. Few people realize that even low inflation of 2 percent or so can reduce purchasing power substantially over a retirement that lasts fifteen years, twenty years, or longer. Your plan needs to anticipate that the price of almost everything you buy in retirement will increase over the years. The mix of goods and services typically purchased by retirees often has a higher inflation rate higher than for goods purchased by pre-retirees.

Evaluate your retirement-income risk profile. Every retirement spending and income strategy has risks. A key to a successful retirement plan is to determine the risks you want to avoid and those with which you're somewhat comfortable and should be able to manage. There are a number of ways to describe the income risks in retirement. I'm going to adapt the descriptions developed by the economist Wade Pfau, who formulated the Retirement Income Style Awareness (RISA) system. He presents some of his work at www.retirementresearcher. com. (See chapter 3 above for more on Pfau's research.)

To determine your retirement income style, you should ask two questions, each of which has two possible answers. Many people aren't fully in one camp or the other on the possible answers. But you're likely to lean more toward one answer than the other.

The first question is: How would you like to receive retirement income? The first choice is probability-based income. Someone who prefers probability-based income wants to invest primarily in the markets and depend on long-term market returns to deliver retirement cash flow. This person is comfortable with the ups and downs of the markets.

The other choice is that you like a safety-first source of retirement income. You prefer income that is delivered according to the terms of contracts, such as pensions, bonds, and annuities. This type of income and cash flow fluctuates less and might not fluctuate at all.

The second question: How much flexibility do you want in retirement-income planning? Choice one is that you like to maintain flexibility. You want to be able to change investments and other plans as circumstances change. Choice two is the opposite: You want to find a solution and lock it in. You won't worry about missing opportunities if the markets or other factors change.

You probably are not fully in one camp or the other on either of these answers. I believe that most people are a blend of these styles and risk profiles—but will lean more toward one than the other.

Four Retirement Spending Models

Today, there are a lot of retirement spending models being used and recommended by financial professionals. (That's a big change from when I first started writing, researching, and advising about retirement finance issues more than thirty years ago.) While there are many models and strategies available, most are variations of each other. The models can be grouped into categories. As with the risk profiles, I'm going to adapt the categories used by Wade Pfau. These are:

Protected income. The protected-income model is for someone who wants safety first and desires little or no optionality. The major sources of protected income are annuities, pensions, and Social Security. In other words, protected income is guaranteed lifetime income.

Time segmentation. This is popularly known as the "buckets strategy," though there are variations of it. A retirement portfolio is divided into segments or buckets. Usually three buckets are used, though a different number is possible. The first bucket is invested in safety-first investments such as money market funds, certificates of deposit, and short-term annuities. This bucket is used to pay for expected retirement spending over the next few years. Usually this bucket has enough money and assets in it to fund two to five years of spending, depending on the degree of safety the owner wants. You're spending both the principal and income from this bucket.

The second bucket is an intermediate-term bucket, which is not meant to be spent until after the period of the safety-first bucket ends. This bucket generally has a five- to-ten-year outlook, and the money in this bucket is invested with moderate risk. The primary goal is to preserve the principal, and the secondary goal is to earn a moderate return.

The third bucket is invested for the long term of ten years and longer. Because this money is invested for the long-term, it can be invested primarily for growth in stocks and other assets that are volatile in the short term but are likely to earn strong returns over time.

Each year or so, money is shifted from the intermediate bucket to the short-term bucket, and from the long-term bucket to the intermediate-term bucket. The amount of risk you're willing to take determines how the portfolio is divided between the intermediate and long-term buckets.

There are many variations of the strategy with different details. Advocates of the time-segmentation approach believe that it reduces the risk a retiree will sell stocks during a market decline, because the retiree knows that several years' worth of spending are safely invested in the short-term bucket.

The Risk Wrap. This strategy combines some of the protection of a contract such as an annuity with the potential for higher returns from investing in the markets. The most common way to implement this approach is to purchase indexed annuities or variable annuities. I won't go into the details of these two types of annuities or other risk-wrap products, which are complicated and have many variations. If the concept sounds appealing you'll need to learn a lot more and work with one or more insurance agents who specialize in these types of annuities before making a decision.

Total return. The total-return approach for generating retirement income, also known as the systematic-withdrawal strategy, is the approach most often recommended by financial planners and other financial professionals.

Under the total-return approach, the retiree's nest egg is invested in a diversified portfolio. The asset allocation may vary from how the retiree was invested during the working years, but the portfolio will be invested based on a combination of the rate of return the retiree wants (or needs) to earn and the risk level he or she is willing to take.

During retirement, the portfolio will generate cash flow from interest, dividends, mutual fund distributions, and perhaps other types of income. The retiree will use that cash flow to pay for living expenses. Additional spending money is generated as needed by selling investments, such as shares of stocks or mutual funds.

The trick to the total-return approach is determining how much money can be distributed from the nest egg each year to fund living expenses without the risk of running out of money later in retirement. The best-known answer is known as the "4 percent rule" or the "safe-spending rate." This strategy is credited to financial planner Bill Bengen, based on a paper he wrote in the 1990s.

Under the 4 percent rule, in the first year of retirement a retiree distributes about 4 percent of his or her nest egg to pay for living expenses. The next year, the dollar amount of the distribution is increased by the inflation rate from the first year of retirement. Each year thereafter, the distribution is the previous year's amount increased by the previous year's inflation rate.

Bengen's research found that under the 4 percent rule a retiree's nest egg would last at least thirty years under a wide range of investment and inflation scenarios. (The success rate exceeded 90 percent but was less than 100 percent.) In fact, the safe first-year distribution rate in the original paper exceeded 4 percent, coming in at 4.6 percent. Over the years, other researchers have verified the results, with the first-year safe spending rate varying between 4 and 5 percent. There have been many criticisms of the 4 percent rule over the years, including some from me. A growing number of people have retirements exceeding thirty years, and the studies don't explore what happens after that point. The portfolio also doesn't last even the full thirty years under all scenarios. A total-return approach takes on a lot of sequence-of-return risk. A total-return approach with a fixed spending formula is great when you retire early in a bull market, but it can cause problems when you retire early in a bear market.

As I explained in the first edition of my book *The New Rules of Retirement*, because both stocks and bonds were in bear markets for much of the 1960s and 1970s, someone who retired in 1966 and used the 4 percent rule would have run out of money before the stock and bond markets entered their great bull markets in 1982.

More recently, critics have pointed out that future investment returns are likely to be lower than those used in the studies by Bengen and others. They argue that the safe-spending rate going forward is more likely to be 3 percent or less. Bengen himself became an advocate for a lower safe spending rate in 2022.[2]

A Flexible Total Return Strategy

I've proposed an alternative total-return approach that is an adaptation of the system the Yale University Endowment uses to determine its annual distributions to the university. I presented details of this method in both editions of *The New Rules of Retirement* and in my newsletter Retirement Watch.

Under the original formula for this method, in the first year of retirement you select a percentage of·the portfolio to spend. Initially I used 4 percent as the first-year spending percentage. Each year after that, you can spend 70 percent of that same percentage of the portfolio's value at the end of the previous year, plus 30 percent of the dollar amount you spent the previous year increased by the previous year's inflation rate.

More recently I modified the model to better reflect how people really spend in retirement, accounting for the Department of Labor data we discussed earlier in this chapter. We saw how people's actual spending in retirement differs significantly from the spending patterns assumed by financial planners' models, including the 4 percent plan. Instead of holding a fixed 4 percent spending rate throughout retirement, the percentage changed over time. In the first six years of retirement, 7 percent is used as the benchmark for spending. It then shifts down to 5 percent beginning in year seven. Finally, the percentage is reduced to 4 percent in the fifteenth year of retirement.

To see how the model would work in a difficult environment, I assumed the entire portfolio was invested in one balanced mutual fund. I compared the results using the actual returns of two mutual funds, with one retiree fully invested in one of the funds and another retiree in the other fund. I used ten years of returns from the mutual funds Vanguard Balanced Index and Vanguard Wellesley Income beginning in 2006. I repeated the ten years of returns so that there would be at least twenty years of returns, and the returns would include two very bad bear markets. The results are in chart 6-1 and chart 6-2, which show the maximum spending amount each year for each of the funds and also the balance at the end of each year.

Under this formula you spend more in the early years of retirement than under the original 4 percent rule. And, as we have seen, that decreasing spending is how many retirees spend their money.

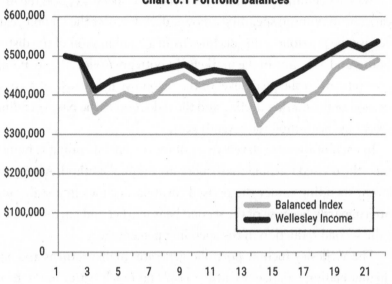

Maximum annual spending from two retirement portfolios, using my modified version of the Yale University Endowment spending formula

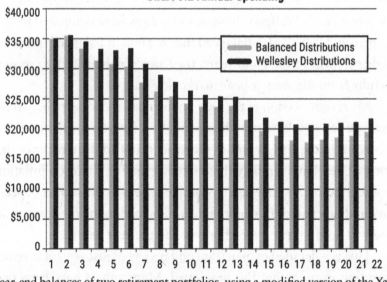

Year-end balances of two retirement portfolios, using a modified version of the Yale University Endowment spending formula

With a beginning $500,000 portfolio, you spend $35,000 the first year. The maximum spending amount declines after the second year, because the portfolio value declines from a combination of the distributions and a decline in the markets. In both portfolios, the spending never returns to the peak level of the second year because of a combination of the market decline and the reduction in the base spending percentage beginning the seventh year.

In each of the first eleven years of retirement, spending is higher under the revised formula than under my original method. After year eleven, spending under the revised formula declines in a stair-step pattern, partly because of the second bear market and partly because of the second reduction in the spending percentage.

The Wellesley Income portfolio generates higher returns and has a higher ending balance because it holds up much better in the bear markets. The Wellesley Income fund is invested about 40 percent in stocks and 60 percent in bonds, while the Wellesley Balanced Index fund is the opposite, 60 percent in stocks and 40 percent in bonds. In the worst years, Wellesley Income lost 9.84 percent compared to over 22 percent for Wellesley Balanced Index. Though Balanced Index has higher returns in the good years, they aren't high enough to recover as fully from the steeper bear market losses.

My revised version of the Yale Endowment spending policy shows that you can develop a spending policy that lets you spend more than 4 percent in the early years of retirement. It also demonstrates that you can develop a strategy that adjusts spending based on inflation, market returns, and changes in your life cycle. Of course, that depends on building enough flexibility into your spending plan—some years you will need to spend less than you did the year before.

This is a detailed explanation and review of just one total-return spending strategy that I've developed. Many others have been proposed. All the total-return approaches are probability-based methods of generating retirement income. They look at past market and economic performance and estimate the probability the methods will work in the future. They also maximize optionality. You maintain control over the investment funds and retain the flexibility to change your investment strategy and seek other opportunities at any time.

How to Choose Your Retirement Spending Strategy

At this point you should have a good idea of the level of retirement spending needed to support your preferred lifestyle in retirement. You also should be deciding whether you lean more toward a probability-based retirement strategy, a safety-first approach, or a strategy that's a combination of the two. Additionally, you should know the extent to which you want flexibility (or optionality) in your strategy and the extent to which you want commitments and contracts in your spending and distribution plan.

The good news is the decisions aren't binary or black and white. You can combine or blend the different strategies to develop a plan with which you are comfortable and that is likely to meet your goals.

I have long recommended that most people consider a blended strategy. Under this strategy, guaranteed lifetime income from Social Security and immediate annuities pays for regular monthly retirement expenses. That way, you know that regardless of what's happening in the markets and economy there will be enough income flowing to your household to meet the spending to support your basic lifestyle. Another strategy, such as one of the total-return approaches, can be used with the rest of your nest egg. That portion will generate income for spending on discretionary and flexible expenses. You can adjust that spending based on the performance of the portfolio, as under the variation of the Yale University Endowment model I recommend, or by using another strategy. In addition, the existence of the guaranteed lifetime income to pay for basic expenses means you can take more investment risk with the rest of the nest egg and potentially earn higher returns than you otherwise would have.

How to Estimate Your Life Expectancy

Using a reasonable estimate of your life expectancy is important to developing a good retirement plan, especially the spending and income strategies. Many retirement decisions should be made with an estimate of life expectancy in mind. For example, someone who has good reason to expect to live less than an average life expectancy probably shouldn't buy either immediate or longevity annuities, but should plan to spend more in the first years of retirement than someone with a longer life expectancy, and should claim Social Security at a younger age.

But many people misunderstand life expectancy and make inaccurate estimates. When a life expectancy estimate is wrong, key decisions about retirement are likely to be less than optimal and the probability of running out of money in retirement rises.

An estimated life expectancy for an age group is properly labeled as "average life expectancy"—the average of all the members of the group. Roughly speaking, about half the members of the age group (which demographers and actuaries call a "cohort") will live longer than the average, and half will have shorter lives. Of the half who will live longer than the average, a meaningful percentage of them will live much longer than the average.

How much longer will the fortunate 50 percent live?

A sixty-five-year-old in the U.S. in 2019 had about a twenty-year life expectancy. That means he or she had a 50 percent probability of living to age eighty-five or longer, according to the Centers for Disease Control. A man aged sixty-five had a life expectancy of just under nineteen years while a woman the same age had a life expectancy of almost twenty-one years. One in four sixty-five-year-old men was expected to live to age ninety-three. Among women aged sixty-five, one in four was expected to live to age ninety-six or older.[3] (Despite a narrowing of the gap in recent years, women are still likely to live several years longer than men.) You can find different estimates from different sources, but they will be similar.

But those are the estimates for the entire age group. Individual life expectancy varies by key factors.

Those who are in good health at age sixty-five need to add an additional two to four years to the group average. People with more education or higher lifetime incomes or both tend to live longer than their age group's average life expectancy. So, if you are in good health, have a college education, and have an above-average lifetime income, you should assume that you'll live years longer than your age-group average, unless there are other factors that could offset those advantages.

Married couples need to consider their joint life expectancy, something that can be significantly different from a single life expectancy. In most married couples, there's a significant probability that at least one spouse will live beyond the average for the age group. In a married couple who are both age sixty-five today, there's a 75 percent probability that at least one spouse will live to age eighty-eight or longer. Age ninety-three for at least one spouse is a 50 percent probability, and there's a 25 percent chance that at least one spouse lives to ninety-eight.

What's Your Longevity Risk?

You shouldn't treat life expectancy as a fixed period. The best we can do is establish probabilities of living to different ages. You need to decide which probability to include in your planning. If there's a 25 percent probability that you or your spouse will live into your nineties, do you want to accommodate that possibility in your plan? Or do you want to assume that's too low a probability to affect your retirement decisions? That's a key question to answer before deciding when to claim Social Security benefits and make other decisions.

Tools You Can Use

There are tools to help develop a reasonable estimate of your life expectancy.

The Society of Actuaries and the American Academy of Actuaries jointly developed an online tool, the Actuaries Longevity Illustrator (ALI). It's available free online at https://www.longevityillustrator. org/. The actuaries sorted through the data and concluded that a reasonable estimate of an individual's life expectancy can be determined from four factors: age, gender, smoking habits, and whether current health is poor, average, or excellent. You enter these factors in the ALI, and it gives you an answer.

The ALI shows your probability of living to different ages. In addition, a couple can enter the data for each individual. The ALI will not only give probable life expectancies for each spouse. It also will answer the questions "How long can we expect to live as a couple?" and "By how many years might one spouse outlive the other?"

There are other individual life-expectancy calculators available free on the internet. One popular calculator is at www.livingto100.com. Social Security has a life-expectancy calculator on its website, and many life insurance companies do also. The calculator by the Wharton School at the University of Pennsylvania has received good reviews. You can access several well-regarded calculators in one place at www.lifeexpectancycalculators.com.

The Tools Have Limits

Online life-expectancy calculators are valuable tools, but they have limits and flaws. Some have more flaws than others. I recommend that if you go this route you use more than one calculator. You'll see different results—they sometimes differ by a decade or more. Then you can decide if you want to be conservative and use the longest projection, average the results, or use another method.

You can also consider one of the scientific services known generally as DNA testing services. You submit some genetic material, usually saliva or blood. You may need to go to a medical lab to submit the sample, though many of these services now use the mail or commercial shipping services. The service will examine your DNA or run blood panels and compare your results to those in its database.

These services once purported to offer a more scientific and personalized estimate of life expectancy than the calculators, but they're largely prohibited now from advertising the life expectancy estimates and downplay them as a result. Some also say they can point to health or medical issues before you display symptoms, or before they are detected by standard tests associated with routine medical exams. Your life expectancy might be extended if you address these issues sooner rather than later.

CHAPTER 7

How to Avoid the Mistakes Most People Make about Medicare and Retirement Medical Expenses

M edical care is one of the largest expenses for most retirees, and one of the top concerns of both retirees and pre-retirees. The top three spending concerns of retirees are the cost of long-term care services, health insurance premiums, and out-of-pocket medical expenses, according to a study on "Retirement Savings and Spending" by T. Rowe Price.[1] About 38 percent of retirees worry they won't be able to obtain affordable medical care in retirement, according to the "21st Annual Transamerica Retirement Survey of Workers."[2]

Some concern about medical expenses in retirement is warranted, but there's no reason for most people to fear that out-of-pocket medical expenses will deplete their nest eggs if they plan properly and make good choices about Medicare and related coverage.

How Much Will It Cost?

Contributing to the worries about retirement medical expenses are estimates of the amount retirees will pay for medical care during retirement. Though intended to help Americans plan for retirement, the studies generate estimates of enormous lifetime costs that intimidate and frighten many people.

The Employee Benefits Research Institute (EBRI) periodically prepares a survey that predicts the amount of money Medicare beneficiaries will need to pay out of pocket for lifetime medical expenses. In 2020, the good news was that the savings target had declined between 8 percent and 10 percent from 2019's forecast.[3] Yet the study predicted that a married couple, each sixty-five years old with median lifetime prescription drug expenses, needed $168,000 in savings to have a 50 percent probability of covering lifetime medical expenses, and $270,000 to have a 90 percent probability of covering their expenses.

A similar study has been issued annually by Fidelity Investments. In 2022 the "Retiree Health Care Cost Estimate" concluded that a different-sex married couple who were each sixty-five years old in 2022 could expect to spend $315,000 in out-of-pocket medical expenses over the next thirty years.[4]

These studies are helpful to an extent, because they let people know that Medicare isn't free and doesn't cover all retirement expenses. But they also cause undue pessimism and worry.

Retirement medical expenses aren't paid in a lump sum, they're paid over a period of years. In addition, the amount you pay out of your pocket depends more on the Medicare coverage you select than on your health. A key to increasing retirement financial security is to limit the amount you pay out of pocket for medical expenses. One industry expert, Katy Votava of goodcare.com, estimates that about 90 percent of Medicare beneficiaries spend more money out-of-pocket than they need to because they don't select the right Medicare coverage.[5] By understanding some basic information about Medicare and taking strategic steps you'll be able to limit your out-of-pocket medical expenses and avoid worrying that retirement medical expenses will deplete your nest egg.

A More Realistic Look at Retirement Medical Spending

A study from the Kaiser Family Foundation (KFF) based on 2016 data from the Centers for Medicare and Medicaid, found that Medicare beneficiaries typically paid $6,000 to $8,000 annually out of pocket for medical expenses. The study also found that a beneficiary in original Medicare with a Medicare supplement (Medigap) policy—see more details about these policies later in the chapter—had higher fixed annual spending because of the premiums but often lower total spending because of the insurance.[6]

If we take a rough average of the KFF numbers and say the average Medicare beneficiary pays $7,000 out of pocket for medical expenses, we have a base estimate of $210,000 total out-of-pocket medical expenses over thirty years. Increase the spending for inflation each year, and the thirty-year total will be around $315,000. You can see how converting the lifetime spending estimate into annual spending makes the expense seem more manageable and less frightening than presenting it as a lump sum that must be in hand at the beginning of retirement.

In the remainder of this chapter, I discuss how to reduce those lifetime retirement medical expenses and, most important, put a limit on the lifetime medical expenses you're likely to pay out-of-pocket. It is the large, unplanned out-of-pocket expenses that concern most people, and many of those expenses can be avoided with good planning.

You'll learn about a key tradeoff: You can try to minimize fixed annual costs, such as premiums for Medicare and related insurance. Doing that, however, leaves you more exposed to the gaps in Medicare, increasing the risk that you'll be responsible for significant medical expenses in case of an illness or injury. You have the choice between limiting the fixed annual costs but taking the risk of being on the hook for large out-of-pocket medical expenses, or else incurring higher fixed annual costs while limiting the potential responsibility for large medical bills.

Breaking Down Retirement Medical Costs

Knowing the different types of medical expenses makes it more likely you'll develop an effective medical insurance plan. The medical expenses that occur during retirement are:

- Premiums, deductibles, and copayments
- Physician and other medical provider visits
- Prescription medications
- Over-the-counter medications and other items
- Hospitalization (including surgery) and all related expenses
- Post-acute care and outpatient services
- Uncovered services: dental, vision, hearing, and long-term care

Keep the different types of medical expenses in mind so you can plan how each will be paid during your retirement.

The Basics of the Medicare Parts

Medicare has several components, known as "parts." You can combine these Medicare parts with coverage offered by the private sector to complete your coverage.

Part A: This part of Medicare covers most expenses related to a hospital admission. It also covers some care received in skilled nursing facilities (also known as nursing homes), hospice care, and home health care. The non-hospital expenses covered under Part A are limited. For example, skilled nursing facility care for up to one hundred days following a stay in a hospital is covered, but additional skilled nursing facility care isn't covered. Most beneficiaries don't pay a premium for Part A.

Part B: Medicare Part B generally covers care received outside of a hospital, including services delivered by doctors or other providers; outpatient care; home health care; durable medical equipment (wheelchairs, walkers, hospital beds, and so forth); and preventive services. Part B also is known as original Medicare or traditional Medicare.

Each beneficiary pays a monthly premium for Part B. There is a base premium that everyone pays, and upper-income beneficiaries pay a higher premium, known as the Medicare premium surtax or IRMAA (Income-Related Monthly Adjustment Amount), which is discussed in chapter 10.

Part B doesn't pay all the costs for the covered care. The most important limit is the 20 percent coinsurance. For many types of care covered by Part B, Medicare pays 80 percent of the total and the beneficiary must pay 20 percent. There is no dollar limit on the coinsurance. The 20 percent coinsurance applies only to Part B, not to the hospital coverage in Part A. An in-depth discussion of the gaps in Part B coverage isn't possible in this book.

Part C: This also is known as a Medicare Advantage plan, a comprehensive alternative to the other parts of Medicare. A beneficiary can choose to enroll in a Part C Medicare Advantage plan instead of original Medicare. How to weigh the tradeoffs between Medicare Advantage and original Medicare and choose which is best for you is discussed later in this chapter.

Part D: Original Medicare did not and still does not cover most prescription drugs. Medicare Part D consists of insurance policies offered by private insurance companies following rules and guidelines set by the Centers for Medicare and Medicaid (CMS). A Medicare Advantage plan incorporates Part D coverage in its benefit package.

Medicare supplement (Medigap): Medigap policies cover gaps in Medicare Parts A and B. These insurance policies, issued by private insurers, are not an official part of Medicare but are regulated by the Centers for Medicare and Medicaid Services (CMS). There are ten different types of Medigap policies. Details of Medicare supplement policies are presented later in this chapter.

Original Medicare versus Medicare Advantage

A Medicare beneficiary's first decision is whether to remain in original Medicare or enroll in a Medicare Advantage plan. The decision can be reconsidered each year during Medicare's open enrollment, but there might be practical limits on the ability to change.

When original Medicare is selected, I strongly encourage the beneficiary to select a package of additional coverage. In addition to Parts A and B, the beneficiary should sign up for a Part D Prescription Drug policy and purchase a Medicare supplement policy.

You'll pay several different premiums: the Part B premium (and possibly the Medicare premium surtax), the Part D premium, and the Medicare supplement premium. The Part B premiums are set by CMS. Insurers set the premiums on Part D and Medicare supplement policies.

Under a Medicare Advantage plan you'll still pay the Part B premium and any Medicare premium surtax that applies to you. Any additional fees are set by the plan. Most Advantage plans charge only a small additional monthly premium or no additional premium.

An Advantage plan provides comprehensive benefits, matching the coverage of Parts A and B as well as Part D prescription drug coverage and the equivalent of Medigap coverage. Many Advantage plans also offer dental, vision, and hearing benefits, which aren't covered at all by Medicare Parts A and B or by Medigap policies. Beneficiaries who elect original Medicare must pay for dental, vision, and hearing care themselves or buy other types of insurance.

An Advantage plan may charge a deductible or copayment for most medical services or prescriptions. The deductibles and copayments vary between plans. Medicare Advantage plans also have annual out-of-pocket spending limits for each member. In 2022, the maximum out-of-pocket spending limit was $6,600.

Under original Medicare you can choose any doctor or other medical provider who accepts Medicare and who will take you as a patient. You don't need approval to see a specialist or receive treatment. Under Medicare Advantage, you receive full coverage only when services are provided by providers in the plan's network, unless it's an emergency. In an Advantage plan, services by a specialist are usually covered only when you receive advance approval. You're also likely to need approval before receiving most procedures and surgeries.

A positive feature of many, but not all, Advantage plans is that care is coordinated by the plan. In original Medicare, the beneficiary is often responsible for choosing the different providers and ensuring that each receives information from the others and has the complete patient picture.

Understanding a Medicare Advantage plan's prescription drug coverage is vital before making a decision. You need to follow the guidelines for selecting a Part D plan later in this chapter to determine if a particular Medicare Advantage is a good match for you.

Under Medicare's rules you can change Medigap (Medicare supplement) policies at any time during the year. But when you're first eligible for Medicare, the insurers who issue Medicare supplement policies are required to sell you the policy of your choice and charge the same premium as for others your age. The insurers can't decline to offer you coverage, limit your coverage, or charge you a higher premium because of pre-existing health conditions. The insurer you select is required to re-enroll you each subsequent year if you choose to stay enrolled, without regard to changes in your health.

After the initial enrollment period, however, insurers aren't required to issue you a new Medigap policy. If you want to shop around for a new Medigap policy or change from a Medicare Advantage plan to original Medicare with a Medigap policy, the insurers can conduct medical underwriting: they can review your medical history and deny coverage or charge a higher premium because of your medical history.

Limits on the ability to switch from Medicare Advantage to original Medicare after the initial enrollment period need to be considered when you are making the initial decision about Medicare coverage.

Find the Best Medigap Policy for You

If original Medicare is your choice, you should buy a Medicare supplement, or Medigap, insurance policy.

As discussed earlier, the biggest gap in Medicare Part B coverage is the 20 percent coinsurance or copayment. Another sizeable gap is in paying some doctor's fees. Medicare reimburses doctors and other medical providers at Medicare's rates, but some doctors that accept Medicare don't accept the reimbursement rate. They're allowed to bill the patients up to an additional 15 percent. You're responsible for that payment, which is known as an excess charge. Another significant gap in Medicare is that it doesn't pay for medical care received outside the United States.

There are other gaps in Part B, which I won't go into detail about here.

Chart 7.1 Medigap Plan Type

Coverage Category	A	B	C	D	F*	G*	K	L	M	N
Part A coinsurance and hospital costs up to an additional 365 days after Medicare benefits are used up	✓	✓	✓	✓	✓	✓	✓	✓	✓	✓
Part B coinsurance or copayment	✓	✓	✓	✓	✓	✓	50%	75%	✓	✓***
Blood (first 3 pints)	✓	✓	✓	✓	✓	✓	50%	75%	✓	✓
Part A hospice care coinsurance or copayment	✓	✓	✓	✓	✓	✓	50%	75%	✓	✓
Skilled nursing facility care coinsurance			✓	✓	✓	✓	50%	75%	✓	✓
Part A deductible		✓	✓	✓	✓	✓	50%	75%	50%	✓
Part B deductible			✓		✓					
Part B excess charges					✓	✓				
Foreign travel exchange (up to plan limits)			80%	80%	80%	80%			80%	80%
Out-of-pocket limit** (in 2022)							$6,620	$3,310		

*Plans F and G also offer a high-deductible plan in some states. With this option, you must pay for Medicare-covered costs (coinsurance, copayments, and deductibles) up to the deductible amount of $2,490 in 2022 before your policy pays anything. (Plans C and F aren't available to people who were newly eligible for Medicare on or after January 1, 2020.)

**For Plans K and L, after you meet your out-of-pocket yearly limit and your yearly Part B deductible, the Medigap plan pays 100% of covered services for the rest of the calendar year.

***Plan N pays 100% of the Part B coinsurance, except for a copayment of up to $20 for some office visits and up to a $50 copayment for emergency room visits that don't result in inpatient admission.

Comparison of the Medicare supplement insurance policies available in 2022

As the nickname implies, a Medigap policy will cover many of the gaps in Medicare Part A and Part B. The policies are offered by private insurers and regulated by the Centers for Medicare and Medicaid Services (CMS). You'll have higher fixed annual costs because you'll pay premiums for the Medicare supplement policy. But you'll have more certainty in your financial planning and will be able to worry much less about out-of-pocket medical bills. You're much less likely to face large unexpected medical expenses that aren't covered by original Medicare.

The key is to find the right Medigap policy for you.

CMS decides which types of Medigap policies can be offered. A policy must conform to one of the types described by CMS, so that all policies of the same type have identical coverage. Insurers can compete only on price, service, history of premium increases, financial stability, and other factors. In addition, you can own only one Medigap policy at a time, and you can't have a Medigap policy if you're in Medicare Advantage.

The ten different types of policies are identified by letter: Plan A, Plan B, and so forth. Chart 7-1 summarizes the different types of policies currently available. In some states there are more or fewer policies than the standard ten, because each state is allowed to modify the CMS rules somewhat, and insurers may decide that some types of policies won't be profitable in a certain area.

Plan G offers the most comprehensive coverage and is the most popular. Plan F used to be the most comprehensive, but Congress prohibited the sale of new Plan F policies after 2019.

Under Plan G, you'll pay the annual Part B deductible, which was $233 in 2022. It's adjusted for inflation each year. After the annual deductible, Plan G pays your share of all Part B–covered charges for the year. The medical provider will bill Medicare, and after Medicare determines how much it will pay for covered services, the Medicare supplement policy pays the rest. If a doctor charges the 15 percent excess charge, the policy will pay that. But the policy won't pay for most services that aren't covered by Medicare Part B, such as dental, vision, and hearing..

In many areas there are multiple insurers offering identical Medigap policies. Highly populated areas can have dozens of policies available. Be sure to shop around. Studies show that premiums on identical policies in the same area can differ by 100 percent. For example, the *Weiss Ratings Medigap Report* annually compiles the rates for plans offered by all Medicare supplement policy issuers and routinely reports substantial differences between premiums for identical policies offered by different insurers. It's available online for a fee. Medicare enables beneficiaries to compare similar policies on its website, and the tool is fairly easy to use for those comfortable with the internet. For Part G Medicap policies available in my area for 2022, the comparison tool on the Medicare website showed that the monthly premiums varied from $102 to $435. Remember, these are policies with identical coverage.

But don't automatically take the policy with the lowest premium. You want an insurer that has been in this market for a long time and has a history of not hitting policyholders with substantial premium increases. The premiums on a Medicare supplement policy are likely to increase every year. But a well-run insurer won't impose significant increases on policyholders. Instead, the increases will be fairly consistent from year to year and in line with medical cost inflation.

You don't need to shop alone. Most localities have one or more insurance agents or brokers who specialize in Medicare coverage. A good agent will review the policies offered by all or most of the insurers in your area. He or she will help determine which policy and insurer best fit your situation. The agent will be paid a commission by the insurer, and the insurer will charge the same premium whether you buy direct after comparing policies through the Medicare website or if you buy through an insurance agent.

An alternative to an insurance agent is the State Health Insurance Assistance Program (SHIP), a free counseling service available to all Medicare beneficiaries and their families. (Some states give it a different name, but each state has the program.) SHIP is funded by federal agencies and run by each of the states. There are no income or wealth limits for using the program. Volunteers are trained to give beneficiaries education and counseling when they are making their medical benefit decisions.

Stop Spending Too Much on Prescription Drugs

Prescription drug spending is expected to increase faster than other categories of medical spending, including medical expenses in general, according to the Kaiser Family Foundation. The foundation found that in a series of five years ending in 2015 the share of Medicare enrollees spending more than $2,000 out of pocket on brand-name prescription drugs almost doubled.[7]

Wise use of a Medicare Part D prescription drug policy or a Medicare Advantage plan can decrease your lifetime out-of-pocket prescription spending. Part D policies are provided by private insurers, but they are regulated by the CMS and subsidized by taxpayers. As discussed above, prescription drug coverage similar to a Part D policy is part of any Medicare Advantage plan. You should shop for a Medicare Advantage plan the same way I describe below to shop for a Part D policy.

You can change Part D policies during Medicare Open Enrollment each year from October 7 to December 15. Some states require Part D insurers to accept any beneficiary who wants to purchase a policy, while others allow insurers to exclude beneficiaries who are looking to switch policies, or to offer different terms to them.

You'll pay a monthly premium for a Part D policy, in addition to regular Medicare Part B and Medicare supplement premiums. But don't buy a policy because it has the lowest premium. You want a policy that leaves you with the lowest total out-of-pocket costs for the year.

The most important feature of any Part D policy is known as the formulary: the list of medicines covered by the plan and how they are classified. A policy might cover only one name-brand drug or require you to try that brand first and cover an alternative only if the first drug doesn't work for you or has side effects. (This is known as step therapy.) Policies also generally cover only a generic drug if both a generic and brand name drug are available, unless you have poor results from the generic.

If you are already taking specific drugs, or if because of your health history you anticipate needing certain drugs in the future, review how they are treated under different policies before making a choice.

Each medication is assigned to a tier. The drugs least expensive to the policyholder—primarily generic drugs—are in tier one, which primarily is generic drugs. The insurer pays all or most of the cost of these drugs. The policyholder pays a greater share of the cost of drugs in higher tiers. The most expensive drugs to the policyholder are in tier four or five. In addition, specialty drugs, experimental drugs, and some high-cost brand name drugs may not be covered at all.

A medication might be tier one or two under one policy and in a higher category under another policy. The categorization is up to each insurer and depends on several factors, the most important of which is usually the pricing agreement the insurer reaches with a drug manufacturer or a pharmacy. You should be aware that an insurer can change a medication's classification from one year to the next (and sometimes even during the year), so it's important to review the plan updates sent to policyholders.

A majority of Part D plans have an initial deductible that you must meet each year before coverage kicks in: you pay the full cost of all your medications until you've met the deductible. But many plans cover Tier 1 and Tier 2 drugs immediately without requiring you to meet the annual deductible.

You might need advance approval before a policy will cover certain drugs. There also may be quantity limits, or a minimum amount of time might have to pass before a prescription can be refilled. A policy may require you to use certain pharmacies to receive maximum coverage.

The CMS has a Part D plan finder tool on the Medicare web site. After opening a personal account on the Medicare web site, you can enter and store details of your medications on the web site and browse different Part D plans. You'll see the prices of the different medications in each plan and an estimate of how much you'll pay out of pocket (including premiums, deductibles, and copayments). I've heard mixed reports about the tool. Some people have said it was helpful, while other have found it difficult to use and complained that the estimates have changed over short periods of time, apparently because of changes in prices for the drugs.

As discussed earlier in this chapter, you can also consult with a local insurance agent or broker who specializes in Medicare, or you can use the SHIP program.

Once you have a policy, stay alert for changes in the formulary and tiers. It is not unusual for an insurer to make changes from year to year for the same policy or even to make changes during the year.

The Part D Coverage Gap or Doughnut Hole

In 2022, Part D Prescription Drug coverage was divided into four stages.

In the first stage, the deductible stage, you pay all the costs until you reach the plan's deductible for the year. The deductible can be up to $480 in 2022, but the insurer can set the deductible at a lower level, and many do. Also, as discussed above, many policies exempt tier 1 and tier 2 drugs coverage from the deductible.

After paying the deductible, you're in the coverage stage. In this stage, you pay a set amount for each prescription. Your share might be a set dollar amount (deductible) or a percentage of the cost (coinsurance).

The third stage is called the coverage gap, doughnut hole, or donut hole. In 2022, the coverage gap began after you and the plan had spent a total of $4,430 on covered drugs. In the coverage gap, you pay no more than 25 percent of the cost of both brand-name and generic drugs. The amount you actually pay out of pocket for generic drugs in this stage counts toward your out-of-pocket expenses. But almost the full cost of brand-name drugs counts as part of your out-of-pocket costs, though you're only paying 25 percent.

After you have spent a total of $7,050 out-of-pocket for prescription drugs in 2022, you leave the coverage gap and enter the catastrophic coverage stage. In this stage you pay no more than 5 percent of the cost of each prescription.

You return to the deductible stage at the start of each calendar year, and the break points of the different stages are adjusted for inflation each year.

The coverage gap will change significantly beginning in 2024 because of changes made by the Inflation Reduction Act, enacted in August 2022.

In 2024, the 5 percent deductible in the catastrophic coverage stage is eliminated. The insured won't pay any more money out of pocket for prescription drugs after reaching the catastrophic coverage level. In 2025 and later years, the coverage gap is eliminated and holders of Part D policies will have their out-of-pocket prescription drug spending capped at $2,000. The $2,000 limit will increase each year after 2025 to match changes in the Consumer Price Index for all urban consumers.

A few other changes to prescription drug spending for Medicare beneficiaries were made in the Inflation Reduction Act. Medicare beneficiaries won't be charged for most vaccines beginning in 2023. For those with Part D policies, their monthly cost for insulin won't exceed $35. In addition, annual premium increases for Part D policies will be limited to no more than 6 percent for the years 2024 to 2029.

Two other provisions are expected to reduce prescription drug costs for beneficiaries over the years. One provision allows the government to negotiate prices for some prescription drugs with the manufacturers, beginning in 2026. In addition, manufacturers of certain drugs will have to pay rebates to the government when the price increase for a medication exceeds the inflation rate.

How to Enroll in Medicare

If you're receiving Social Security retirement benefits before age sixty-five, the Social Security Administration (SSA) will automatically enroll you in Parts A and B of Medicare. Shortly before your sixty-fifth birthday you'll receive a Medicare card and other information in the mail. If you don't want to be enrolled in Medicare at that time (say, because you're working and covered by a qualified employer plan), you can contact the SSA and withdraw your application for Medicare.

If you aren't yet receiving Social Security retirement benefits, you need to apply for Medicare near your sixty-fifth birthday. You can apply by making an appointment at the nearest Social Security office or by calling the SSA's toll-free number, but the easiest way to apply is to open a mySocialSecurity account on the SSA's web site. Then log in, find the Medicare application link, and complete the application. It should take only a few minutes. The SSA will notify you in a week or two that you have been enrolled and provide your Medicare numbers.

When to Enroll in Medicare

You'll pay substantially more for the coverage if you don't enroll when first eligible and then decide to enroll later. You'll pay higher premiums for the rest of your life, not a one-time penalty. In addition, insurers aren't required to issue a Medicare supplement policy after your initial enrollment period has passed. You could be denied the Medicare supplement insurance or pay a higher premium for it.

Enroll in Medicare when you're first eligible, unless you qualify for one of the exceptions to the penalties for enrolling later, discussed below.

The Initial Enrollment Period

Your initial enrollment period for Medicare will occur before your full retirement age for Social Security, so don't confuse Medicare enrollment with claiming Social Security benefits. You're eligible for Medicare when you turn age sixty-five—and you can actually sign up a little earlier than that: three months before the first day of the month of your sixty-fifth birthday.

There's no premium for Part A of Medicare, and there's no penalty for signing up late.

The initial enrollment period for Part B is a seven-month period that is centered on the month you turn sixty-five. Your sixty-fifth birthday month and the three months before and the three months after that birthday month are the initial enrollment period. (With one wrinkle: anyone with a birthday on the first day of the month is treated as having been born in the previous month.) At any time during that period you can enroll in Medicare Part B without penalty and also buy a Medicare supplement policy without any medical underwriting or qualifications.

In order to enroll in a Medicare Advantage plan (Part C of Medicare, the alternative to the original Medicare), you must first enroll in Part B. So, the initial enrollment period for Medicare Advantage plans is the same as for original Medicare. And so is the initial enrollment period for Medigap (Medicare Supplement) policies.

New Medicare coverage always starts on the first of the month. If you apply for Part B or Part C at least a month before you turn sixty-five, then the coverage will begin on the first day of the month in which you turn sixty-five. If you apply during the month you turn sixty-five, or in any of the subsequent three months, coverage won't begin until the first day of the month after you apply.

An Exception to the Part B Initial Enrollment Period

Your initial enrollment period is delayed when you are covered by a "qualified medical expense" plan when you turn sixty-five. A qualified medical expense plan is a group plan through an employer (or a former employer, if you receive retirement medical benefits) with twenty or more employees.

A self-employed person or someone who is working for (or retired from) an employer with nineteen or fewer employees doesn't qualify for the exception. Also, be aware that any COBRA continuation coverage you have through a former employer doesn't qualify you for the exception, even if current active employees qualify for the exception. Check with your plan administrator if you have any questions about whether the coverage applies for the exception.

If you're married and receive medical insurance through your spouse's employer, and that coverage qualifies for the exception, then you also qualify for the exception. Once your spouse leaves the employer or you lose that coverage for any reason, your initial enrollment period begins.

Once you lose the qualified medical coverage that delayed your initial enrollment period you have eight months to sign up for Medicare. That is your new initial enrollment period.

An Exception to the Part D Initial Enrollment Period

You can also avoid the penalty for signing up for Medicare Part D late if you have "creditable drug coverage" during your initial enrollment period. After losing creditable drug coverage for any reason, you have up to sixty-three days to sign up for a Part D policy or obtain other creditable drug coverage.

Creditable drug coverage is prescription medication coverage that provides similar value or coverage as a Part D policy. It can be provided by a current or former employer, TRICARE, Indian Health Service, the Veterans Administration, or an individual policy. If you have any doubts, check with your prescription medication insurer or plan administrator.

The Penalties for Late Enrollment in Medicare Parts B and D

After missing the initial enrollment period, you can enroll in Medicare only during the general enrollment period from January 1 to March 31 each year. The coverage you sign up for during that period takes effect on July 1 of that year. Thus one penalty of delaying beyond your initial enrollment period is that you are without Medicare coverage for an extended time.

The financial penalty is that every month for the rest of your life the Part B premium is increased 10 percent for each full twelve-month period that you could have been enrolled in Part B but weren't. Because the penalty is a percentage of the Part B premium, and the Part B premium is almost certain to increase over time, you'll pay a higher penalty each year.

Only full twelve-month periods count when computing the penalty. For example, if you don't sign up for Medicare until twenty-seven months after the end of your initial enrollment period, your penalty is 20 percent, based on only two full 12-month periods of late enrollment.

When you sign up for Part D prescription drug policy outside of the initial enrollment period, your premium is increased 1 percent per month for each month you could have signed up for Part D but didn't. A full twelve-month delay results in a 12 percent penalty. That penalty continues for the rest of your life if you have a Part D prescription drug policy.

The 1 percent penalty isn't based on your own Part D premium for the plan you select. Instead, it is 1 percent of the "national base beneficiary premium," which is similar to an average of premiums on Part D policies available that year. The national base beneficiary premium was $33.06 in 2021 and $33.37 in 2022.

In addition, if you fail to sign up for a Part D policy during your initial enrollment period, you can't apply for a policy until the next open enrollment period, which runs from October 15 through December 7 each year.

The Penalty for Late Enrollment for a Medicare Supplement

There is no specific financial penalty for seeking a Medigap (Medicare supplement) policy outside your initial enrollment period. But when you apply for a Medicare supplement policy outside your initial enrollment period, insurers aren't required to issue you a policy. Insurers can engage in medical underwriting: they can examine your medical history and records, and you can be denied coverage or charged a higher premium because of underlying health conditions.

How Much Should It All Cost?

If you opt for original Medicare plus the additional coverage I recommend, these are the different types of recurring medical expenses you can expect to have in retirement.

Part B premium: The base Part B premium in 2022 was $170.10 per month. Higher-income beneficiaries will owe higher premiums because of the Medicare premium surtax, or IRMAA, discussed in Chapter 10.

Part D premium: The average premium for Part D in 2022 was $43 per month. The Part D policy also may have a deductible. The average deductible in 2022 was $435.

Medicare supplement (Medigap) premium: Most new Medicare beneficiaries are able to obtain a Plan G policy for about $200 per month, though premiums vary considerably. The premiums will increase annually with medical inflation.

Non-covered expenses: The most common uncovered medical expenses are vision, dental, and hearing. Mental health coverage may be limited or excluded under both original Medicare and Medigap policies. You can seek additional coverage for these expenses or plan to pay for them out of pocket. In most areas you'll find that vision and dental policies, whether they are insurance or discount plans, aren't worth the cost.

Some prescription drug expenses won't be covered by Medicare D even after you meet the annual deductible. The details vary from policy to policy. There may be deductibles or copayments on each prescription. You'll pay a higher share of the cost of some drugs than of others. You may find yourself in the coverage gap ("doughnut hole"), in which you pay a higher share of the costs.

A ballpark number: Under original Medicare, in 2022 you would have paid a minimum of $2,041.20 for Part B premiums. The average Part D premium was $43 per month, or another $516.00 annually. A Medicare supplement (Medigap) plan with a premium of $200 per month would be another $2,400 for the year.

That's a total of just under $5,000 for the insurance premiums. Deductibles would total at least $500 for both Part B and Part D. After that, most hospital and doctor expenses and a large portion of prescription drug expenses should be covered by the policies.

Dental, vision, and hearing costs vary considerably from individual to individual. On average, a retiree with this package of coverage is likely to pay $8,000 to $10,000 annually out of pocket for medical care. Some will spend more, especially those who incur substantial dental or vision care or need hearing aids.

Medicare is individual coverage only. There is no family or spouse coverage under Medicare. If you're married, your spouse will pay his or her own premiums and out-of-pocket expenses, effectively doubling the numbers above for a married couple.

Under a Medicare Advantage Plan

If you choose a Medicare Advantage plan instead of original Medicare, you'll still pay the Part B premium plus any additional amount due under the Medicare premium surtax. Many Advantage plans don't charge an additional monthly premium, or they charge only a nominal amount, but some charge $200 or more per month. An Advantage plan might charge a copayment of $5 to $20 for each doctor's visit and for most other services.

All Advantage plans have an annual out-of-pocket limit or maximum out of pocket (MOOP). In 2022, the MOOP was $6,700 for most plans.

A Medicare Advantage plan usually offers some level of dental, vision, and hearing coverage. But the extent of the coverage varies, and you're limited to providers who are part of the plan's network.

Most Advantage plan members will pay less out of pocket than original Medicare beneficiaries if they don't need much medical care. But that's not the case when an Advantage plan member incurs enough expenses to hit the MOOP. In those situations, original Medicare with Medicare supplement and Part D policies usually turns out to be less expensive.

Be Sure to Shop Around

No matter which route you choose to go for your Medicare coverage package, be sure to shop around. Though many of the coverages are identical and there may be only small differences between policies, the cost may vary considerably, as you can see by scrolling through the Medicare Plan Finder tool on the Medicare web site. Or you can review some of the research on Medicare plan pricing.

You don't want to buy solely on the basis of the lowest premium, but you do want to shop around. You don't want to overpay for coverage because you didn't shop around but simply bought the policy that was advertised the most or that a friend has. If you don't compare prices, your premiums could be 100 percent or more above what you need to pay for a quality policy from a quality insurer.

CHAPTER 8

Who Will Change My Light Bulbs?
How to Sort through the Confusion and Chaos in Long-Term Care

The potential that long-term-care expenses may diminish their nest eggs and the financial legacies they leave is a major worry of many Americans. Yet, Americans don't want to talk about or even contemplate long-term care (LTC), much less plan for it. One of every four adults would rather go to the dentist than talk about LTC, according to a 2014 survey by Genworth, a leading issuer of LTC insurance.[1]

More important, misinformation and misunderstandings abound about LTC and how to plan for it. I could quote many surveys that show widespread misunderstanding about what LTC is, how likely someone is to need it, how much LTC could cost, and how to plan to finance any LTC care that may be needed in the future. Complicating the situation is the fact that the LTC insurance industry has been in upheaval since 2008, with many insurers leaving the market and others increasing premium substantially, while reducing benefits.

None of this should deter you from developing an LTC strategy that fits your needs and situation and establishing it as part of your retirement plan. In this chapter, I present the facts about LTC and show how to create an LTC plan.

Many people assume that family will be available to help with any care they need. But relying on family, even a spouse, can be a mistake. Even when family members are willing to assume a caregiver role, that doesn't mean they'll be able to fulfill the role. Other family members might not live nearby or might not be able to take time from their families and jobs to provide the care. No one can know if he or she will need LTC, and more importantly, no one can know the type of care that they will need.

When family members do help with LTC, being a caregiver often presents significant strains on them. It increases their stress levels, which can ultimately contribute to both physical and mental health problems. Many family caregivers put their own careers and other family obligations aside and earn lower income. They often use some of their own financial resources as part of the caregiving. This can be manageable when the caregiving lasts for a few months, but you can't know how long the need for care will last. LTC could be needed for years and that could devastate the health and finances of the caregivers.

Having an LTC plan can protect financial assets for both you and your children. You probably want to avoid becoming financially dependent on others and especially want to avoid having your children's income and assets being spent on your LTC.

The Need for Long-Term Care

If you have investigated long-term at all, you have probably heard that 70 percent of those sixty-five and over will need some kind of

LTC during their lifetimes. That's a widely quoted statistic, and it comes from a U.S. government report issued some years ago.[2] It is also misleading.

The need for long-term care is defined in most LTC insurance (LTCI) policies and in the LTC business generally as having a cognitive impairment or needing help with at least two of the six activities of daily living (ADL). The six ADLs are bathing, dressing, personal hygiene and grooming, eating, toileting, and transferring or mobility.

Though it's called long-term care, the definition doesn't say anything about how long the conditions last or the care is needed. That's where the 70 percent statistic is misleading. Many people at some point in their lives need help with at least two of the ADLs. But for many the need is temporary. Someone who has a major surgery or an illness often goes into a hospital and subsequently needs help with some of the ADLs as they recover and are sent from the hospital to a nursing home or rehabilitation facility where they receive full-time care and perhaps physical therapy—until they no longer need help with at least two of the ADLs. A person might need help with the ADLs for a few days or weeks, and then be sent home. The help isn't needed long term, and yet it qualifies as LTC under the prevailing definition. That's where the 70 percent number comes from.

The stereotype is that LTC will be delivered in a nursing home, often referred to today as a skilled nursing facility (SNF) or acute care facility. But LTC now is delivered in a variety of environments.

Assisted-living residences (ALRs) have expanded greatly in the United States, and many people who would have gone into nursing homes in the past now reside in ALRs. An ALR is for people who need less medical care. It is often said that a nursing home is a medical model of care while an ALR is a social model. In many states ALRs are regulated and monitored by a social services agency, while nursing homes are regulated by a medical agency. Most ALRs also have separate sections known as memory care units. In these units, care is provided for people with different levels of cognitive impairment.

Adult day care is also considered long-term care, and its cost is covered by most LTC insurance policies.

Home care is another form of LTC, and it is growing in popularity. Of those with long-term care insurance policies, about 73 percent of initial claims in 2021 were for LTC received at home, according to the American Association of Long-Term Care Insurers.[3]

Both personal care and medical care can be delivered at a person's home. A home-care aide can periodically help with chores such as cleaning and preparing meals and also with dressing and other personal activities.

Home medical care aides can perform a range of tests, procedures, and care at a person's home. While Medicare and other medical insurance policies do not pay for the cost of the long-term care, they will pay for the cost of medical equipment that the medical care aide can use in the home.

How Likely Are You to Need LTC, Really?

One way to assess how likely you are to need LTC is to review data from the American Association of Long-Term Care Insurers (AALTCI). The data should be used with some caution, because it comes from companies that sell some form of LTCI and doesn't reflect the full population. But the data is important to consider and should help to inform your decisions.

In its data for 2021, the AALTCI reported that of people who had bought LTCI at age 65, 50 percent used their policy benefits during their lifetimes. On average 171 months, or 14 years, passed before a policyholder claimed benefits. The data also show that among married couples, after one spouse claims LTC benefits, the other spouse is much more likely than the average person to claim LTC benefits and usually claims them within one year after the other spouse claimed benefits or passed away.

How Long LTC Will Be Needed

Many people can pay the cost of LTC for a few months or even a year or two. What people fear is the multi-year need for LTC. The AALTCI data say that about 27 percent of claims are for one year or less. Benefits are claimed for one to two years by 19 percent of policyholders, and 14 percent claim for two to three years. About 10 percent claim benefits for three to four years, 8 percent for four to five years, and 6 percent for five to six years. Only 10 percent need LTC for more than six years.[4]

How Much Does LTC Cost?

The cost of LTC depends on the type of care received and where it is received. The cost varies around the country and even among different parts of a state. Cost also varies among individual providers.

But it can be useful to look at average costs to develop a benchmark for the potential cost of LTC. The most widely quoted source of costs is an annual survey from Genworth, the leading issuer of traditional LTCI policies in the U.S. The results are published on its website. Another source is the AALTCI, which publishes more limited data on its web site.

In its 2021 survey, Genworth found the following median national monthly costs for LTC services:

Home care aide (homemaker services)	$4,957
Home health aide	$5,148
Adult day health care	$1,690
Assisted living residence	$4,500
Nursing home, semi-private room	$7,908
Nursing home, private room	$9,034

The Genworth survey also breaks down costs by locality, calculating median costs by state and for some of the more populous regions in many states.[5]

When looking at estimates and quotes, keep in mind that the daily cost quoted by most LTC providers is only the basic cost. Many people who need LTC also need some care and services in addition to the basic services covered by the basic daily cost. Those additional costs might be paid by Medicare if they are medical services, but in many cases they are personal services Medicare doesn't cover. I've heard estimates that in assisted living residences and nursing homes the average person receives additional services that are about 20 percent over the basic daily cost.

Medicare Won't Help

Medicare pays for LTC only under limited circumstances. Medicare will pay for up to one hundred days of LTC if the care immediately follows a hospital stay of more than three consecutive days. But if you still need help with at least two of the ADLs after the first hundred days, Medicare won't pay for the care. And if you need long-term care without having been in a hospital first (which is the case for most LTC care), Medicare won't pay for any of the LTC.

Medicaid Is a Long Shot

Medicaid is the federal government program that pays for medical care for people with low incomes and few assets. It pays for a high percentage of the country's total nursing home costs, but most people don't want to plan on Medicaid paying for their LTC costs.

First, Medicaid pays only nursing home expenses. It doesn't pay for assisted living care. In some states Medicaid is expanding payments for home LTC, but this coverage still is limited.

More important, to qualify you must meet Medicaid's definition of being impoverished. The rules have been tightened several times over the years to limit the ability of middle class and upper middle class people to game the system to qualify for Medicaid while keeping their assets in the family. Generally, you must give away most of your assets and sources of income at least five years before you plan to apply for Medicaid benefits. I won't go into details of Medicaid qualification strategies. If you want to consider this route, be sure to work with an attorney who's experienced in this area and has successfully helped people qualify for Medicare's LTC benefits.

Should You Self-Fund LTC?

Based on the data from AALTCI, to self-fund you should have enough income and assets to pay for at least three years of LTC. In the data, a high percentage of LTC benefit claims are for three years or less, and a small percentage are for more than five years.

But it's not enough to have wealth. You should have cash or assets that can be converted to cash. There are a number of people who are fairly wealthy, but their wealth isn't liquid. It might be in small businesses, investment real estate, or some other illiquid assets. You don't want to be in a situation in which such assets have to be sold quickly to fund long-term care.

Many people assume they'll be able to use their home equity to pay for LTC. That's correct if they plan to sell the home and move to a residence that provides LTC, such as assisted living. But now more than half of America's seniors say they want to receive any LTC at home. You can't receive care at home if a sale of the home is needed to fund the care. You might be able to receive LTC at home and use the home equity to pay for the care by taking out a reverse mortgage, but only a portion of the home equity will be available to pay for the LTC, and the home equity that pays for the LTC and reverse mortgage costs won't be available for others to inherit. (See chapter 12 for details about reverse mortgages.) Also, if all or most of the home equity is used to pay for home care using a reverse mortgage and you eventually need to move into an ALR or other facility, there won't be any home equity available to pay for continued care.

If you're married, keep in mind that you should have enough wealth to pay for LTC for each spouse. Also, there's a good possibility one spouse will need LTC and the other won't. In those cases, the marital residence might have to be maintained for one spouse while the other resides in assisted living or other LTC.

How to Insure against the Potential Need for Long-Term Care

As with many other uncertain risks, there's insurance to help pay for LTC you might need. Of course, you have to buy the insurance before you might need it, preferably long before you might need it. Insurers have become more rigorous in their underwriting over the years. LTCI has been around in the United States only since about the 1970s. For years insurers underestimated the life expectancy of their policyholders and the percentage of them who would claim benefits. They now have more data and are correcting those errors.

Because of the changes, insurers are more likely to deny coverage to applicants with pre-existing conditions that are likely to lead to future LTC needs. Data from AALTCI and others over the years indicates that the percentage of applicants denied LTCI has increased. Age is also a factor. The older you are the more likely you are to be denied LTCI. If you're interested in LTCI, apply when you're in your fifties or your sixties, and the earlier the better. The longer you wait, the more likely you are to have a condition that could cause your coverage to be denied.

Different Types of Long-Term Care Insurance

There are two main types of LTCI to consider. There is the traditional stand-alone LTCI, much like auto or homeowner's insurance. You pay premiums for protection against a certain risk, in this case the need for LTC. If you never need LTC and don't qualify for and claim benefits, you and your heirs receive nothing from the policy other than the peace of mind of knowing the coverage was in place. If you qualify for benefits, the policy pays under its terms. Traditional LTCI is sometimes known as "use-it-or-lose-it" coverage. You pay the premiums but might never receive any benefits or payments from the policy.

The other type of LTCI is called hybrid LTCI, asset based LTCI, linked LTCI, or combination coverage. The coverage goes by these names because it isn't a stand-alone LTCI policy. Instead, this type of coverage is a traditional annuity or permanent life insurance policy with long-term coverage attached, usually as a rider. There are many variations of this type of LTCI, and I'll be able to discuss them only generally.

Since 2008, sales of traditional stand-alone LTCI have fallen dramatically. AALTCI says over seven hundred thousand such policies were sold in its peak year of 2000. Since then, sales have declined, and the decline accelerated after 2008. In 2020, only forty-nine thousand traditional LTCI policies were sold. At the same time, sales of the hybrid policies accelerated. Over six hundred thousand were in force at the end of 2019, according to AALTCI.

The Troubles in Traditional LTCI

Insurers made a number of assumptions when determining the premiums for policies that were sold from the 1980s through to the financial crisis that occurred around 2008, and many of these assumptions turned out to be inaccurate.

Far fewer policyholders let their policies lapse after paying premiums for a few years than the insurers had expected. That factor, combined with longer life expectancies, caused a higher percentage of policyholders to file claims than the insurers expected. Plus, the cost of LTC rose faster than the insurers anticipated.

Low interest rates also hurt the insurers. Insurers collect and invest premiums for years before paying benefits on LTCI policies. As interest rates on bonds and other investments declined, returns to many insurers declined below the insurers' expectations.

Many insurers left the LTCI market. While there were one hundred or more insurers offering the policies a couple of decades ago, there now are only about a dozen, and a small number of them account for most of the new policy sales.

Many insurers that didn't leave the traditional LTCI market raised premiums. Insurers increased premiums on existing policyholders, with a few policyholders facing one-year increases of 40 percent or more after 2008. On new policies, insurers reduced the coverage available, making the policies less attractive to potential new clients. Unlimited lifetime coverage has essentially been eliminated. Most insurers will provide coverage for no more than three or five years. Unlimited inflation indexing of benefit limits also isn't available any longer. Traditional LTCI policies now have dollar limits on both annual and lifetime benefits.

How Much Does Traditional LTCI Cost?

The cost of LTCI varies considerably between insurers and based on several other factors. It's important to shop around, because different insurance companies charge very different premiums for identical policies to people of the same age, and even living in the same area. In its annual "LTCI Facts," cited earlier, AALTCI usually shows the difference between the highest and lowest premiums in addition to the median premiums. In 2021, among policies purchased at age fifty-five, the premiums for male customers differed by 71 percent. For females it was 60 percent, and for couples it was 52 percent.

Another cost factor is how an insurer classifies your current health status. "Preferred" is the best health status and carries the lowest premiums. Someone with "Select" health status still is insurable but will be charged higher premiums than a Preferred individual. Insurers have different standards for determining who is classified in each status.

With those caveats, here are samples from 2021 of some average annual premiums for LTCI policies with an initial lifetime benefit limit of $165,000, according to the American Association for Long-Term Care Insurance. You can see the latest data at the AALTCI website.

For a single male at age fifty-five, the annual premium was $950 if the policy had no growth in benefits, or inflation indexing. With 2 percent annual growth in benefits, the annual premium was $1,750, and with 5 percent annual growth in benefits, the annual premium was $3,685. For a single female aged fifty-five, annual premiums for the same policies were $1,500, $2,815, and $6,400. For joint coverage of a married couple, the annual premiums were $2,080, $3,870, and $8,575.

To see how premiums vary with age, let's look at the same policies purchased at age sixty-five.

For the single male, the first-year premiums for the different policies were $1,700, $2,600, and $4,200. For a female policyholder, the premiums were $2,700, $4,230, and $7,225. And for joint coverage of a couple, the premiums were $3,750, $5,815, and $9,675 if both were sixty-five years old.[6]

Those are the first-year premiums. Insurers expect future premium increases to be more in line with annual inflation, rather than the large premium increases that many insurers imposed following 2008.

The Hybrid Revolution

Sales of hybrid LTCI policies rose rapidly from almost zero just a few years ago to five hundred thousand in 2015 and more than six hundred thousand in 2019. It's understandable why the policies are rising in popularity. The troubles with traditional LTCI after 2008 made it unattractive, many people looked for alternatives, and the hybrid policies were the alternative available.

A hybrid policy starts as either a traditional annuity or a permanent life insurance policy. The insured elects a rider that pays benefits if LTC is needed. The policy is usually purchased with a lump-sum deposit. Under the terms of these policies and riders, the maximum lifetime LTC benefit exceeds the deposit the insured made to purchase the policy; it can be anywhere from twice to ten times or more of the deposit. The amount of the maximum benefit depends on the type of policy purchased: its details, the age of the insured, and when the LTC benefits are claimed. In the annuities with LTC riders, the insured's deposit earns interest each year, and in many of them the LTC benefit also increases as the interest increases the account balance.

The insured's ability to withdraw the interest or the principal without penalty is usually limited during the first years after the annuity is acquired. But after a period of time the annuity can be liquidated without penalty. Of course, taking a withdrawal reduces the amount of LTC benefits, and liquidating the policy ends them. An important feature for many is that if the insured keeps the annuity and never needs the LTC benefits, after he or she passes away the beneficiaries named by the insured receive the annuity balance—only the deposit plus compounded interest, not the amount of the maximum LTC benefits.

In the permanent life insurance version of a hybrid LTCI policy, the amount of the LTC benefit is a multiple of the deposit made to acquire the policy. The policy also has a cash value account. As the cash value increases over time, the maximum LTC benefit usually increases. In addition, the insured can usually take money out of the cash value account if needed. If the insured never needs LTC or doesn't need it for long, the beneficiaries of the policy receive the life insurance benefit after the insured passes away. (The life insurance benefits are less than the maximum LTC benefits.)

One reason the policies can offer LTC benefits that exceed the deposit used to acquire a policy is that when LTC is needed the insured's account balance or cash value is first used to pay for LTC. Suppose $100,000 is deposited in an annuity that has a rider with $250,000 of LTC benefits. When the annuity owner needs long-term care, the LTC benefits paid to him or her first reduce the principal and accumulated interest in the annuity account. If the owner passes away before that amount is exhausted, the beneficiary receives the remaining principal and interest, if any. But if the annuity owner is paid LTC benefits that exceed the principal plus accumulated interest, there is nothing left for the beneficiary.

The permanent life insurance with an LTC rider works in a similar way. LTC benefits first reduce the cash value account and the life insurance benefits of the policy.

Under the hybrid policies, when the insured qualifies for LTC benefits, the benefit payments are usually made in fixed monthly amounts stated in the policy contract; the payments aren't related to how much the insured is paying for the care.

In addition, there are no restrictions on how the benefit payments can be used. The insured can use them for any type of LTC once the qualifications are met: either they require help with at least two of the ADLs, or they are cognitively impaired. The insured can even use the benefits to pay a relative or friend to provide help in the home, make gifts to family members, or anything else. For example, if the monthly benefit payment exceeds what the policy owner pays for LTC, the excess can be saved for the future.

This highlights an important difference between traditional and most hybrid LTCI. Traditional policies are reimbursement policies, while most (though not all) hybrid policies are not. With a reimbursement policy, once the insured qualifies for benefits, the insurance company reimburses the insured for actual LTC expenses. The insured, or the insured's representative, present long-term-care bills to the insurance company. The company reviews them, decides the expenses that are reimbursable as LTC, and reimburses the insured. Or the process may be streamlined so that LTC provider sends bills directly to the insurer.

In an indemnity policy (which is what most of the annuity and permanent life insurance policies are), the insured is sent a monthly payment of a fixed amount after meeting the qualifications for LTC benefits. The amount of the payment isn't related to costs incurred by the insured, and the insurance company doesn't review any bills.

There is a large variety of hybrid policies. It is best to work with an experienced LTCI advisor, whether an insurance broker, financial planner, or estate planner. The advisor should work with a number of insurance companies and review their offerings instead of being committed to one or a small number of insurers and their products. If you can't find such an advisor, the best alternative is to work with several different insurance agents or brokers so that among them you are seeing most of the available market for LTCI.

Customize Your LTCI

Whether you choose traditional LTCI or one of the hybrids, the details of the LTC coverage matter, and the details to pay attention to are the same for all the policies. They can usually be modified so that you have the best coverage for your goals and budget.

Coverage triggers: Almost all LTCI policies now have standardized coverage triggers. The insured qualifies for benefits after help is needed with at least two of the ADLs or when there is cognitive impairment. Most insurers accept a certification from any licensed medical professional, and the professional can be either a medical doctor or a nurse. Some insurers contract with medical professionals around the country who will see the insured, review the medical records, and determine whether he or she qualifies for LTC.

Indemnity or reimbursement: The difference between these two methods of paying benefits is reviewed above. Decide if the difference is important to you and, if so, consider only policies with the form of benefit payment that you want.

The amount of the daily or monthly benefit: Traditional LTCI policies and other reimbursement policies have a daily maximum benefit amount. The insured is reimbursed for the qualified expenses incurred up to the maximum daily benefit amount for each day that LTC is needed. Indemnity policies pay a fixed amount, which usually is expressed as a monthly or daily amount.

A reimbursement policy often has different daily benefit amounts for the different types of care received. Nursing home care usually pays the highest daily benefit, while day care pays the lowest benefit. Hybrid policies and some traditional LTCI policies generally provide a single monthly benefit amount regardless of the type of LTC the insured receives.

You need to be aware of the benefit amounts under a policy and compare them to the costs of the different types of care in your area or the area where you're likely to receive LTC.

Also, adjusting the benefit amount is one way to make LTCI affordable, especially in traditional LTCI. A standard policy might have benefit amounts based on the median cost nationally, in your area, or determined by some other basis. If you conclude that Social Security benefits and some other sources of income can pay for part of your LTC, you can elect to reduce the daily or monthly benefit amount in the policy, and that will reduce the cost of the policy.

A hybrid policy and other indemnity policies usually determine the daily or monthly benefit amount by the amount of the deposit you make to acquire the policy.

The deductible: An LTCI policy might refer to a deductible, elimination period, or waiting period. Even after it is determined that you need LTCI, insurance benefits don't begin right away. The insurer won't make payments until after the elimination, or waiting, period which might be called a deductible. You must pay all the cost of LTC for a certain period before the insurance policy benefits kick in.

Before the financial crisis, it was possible to find policies with no waiting period. Those policies aren't available to new purchasers now, and you'll have a tough time finding a policy with an elimination period of less than ninety days. That's true of both traditional and hybrid LTCI policies.

You can select a different waiting period and use it to lower your LTCI costs. You might decide that you're able and willing to pay all the costs of LTC for longer than ninety days, perhaps up to one year. You can adjust the waiting period to up to 365 days. That will dramatically reduce the cost of the insurance and make it more affordable to you. It also means you're buying insurance that will pay benefits only if you need LTC for more than one year.

But before doing that, compare the cost of LTC for one year to how much the cost of the insurance is with the longer elimination period. You might find that the premium savings aren't enough to justify paying for the care for the length of the longer elimination period.

Maximum benefit period or lifetime benefit amount: LTCI policies will pay benefits only for a maximum number of years, usually three or five years, or else only up to a maximum lifetime dollar amount.

The insurer generally allows you to choose the benefit period or benefit amount within limits and sets the premium or deposit based on your choice. When shopping for a policy, ask to see the premiums for different benefit periods or amounts. A shorter maximum benefit period could make the policy more affordable. Or selecting a shorter benefit period could let you select a higher daily or monthly benefit.

Inflation protection: We saw earlier that the average person buys LTCI about fourteen years before claiming benefits under the policy, according to AALTCI data. The cost of LTC is going to increase during that period, and it's probably going to increase at a higher rate than general consumer price inflation. A policy benefit that was adequate when the policy was purchased covers only a fraction of the cost of LTC when benefits are paid fourteen years or more later.

That's why LTCI policies allow you to select inflation protection, also known as a benefit growth factor. You can select a fixed rate at which the benefit amount will increase each year. The rate usually can be 1 percent up to 5 percent, at increments of one percentage point.

The higher the growth factor, the higher the premiums. You need to select a growth rate that balances the cost of the insurance with the amount you'll have to self-insure if LTC is needed. One strategy some advisors recommend is to select a higher initial benefit amount and a lower growth rate. That often results in a lower cost than selecting a lower initial benefit amount with a higher growth rate.

Covered care: LTCI is no longer just "nursing home insurance." An LTCI policy should cover LTC no matter where or how it is received. It should cover adult day care, home care (both personal and medical care), assisted living, memory care, and nursing home care (or skilled nursing facility care). Don't buy a policy that doesn't cover at least those types of care. Also, look closely at the definitions. Some policies say they cover only home care provided by licensed professionals, which means they won't cover care such as cooking and cleaning. They'll cover only medical-related care or care by medical providers with a professional license.

Some policies will pay for care provided by family or friends, at least under some circumstances. Other policies won't.

Use the information about policy provisions above to make sure you purchase a policy that's going to cover the LTC you might need and not leave you with substantial gaps. Also customize the policy so it delivers the maximum care you can afford and doesn't charge you for care you don't think you're likely to need or don't want to pay for.

Other Key Factors

There are some other factors to consider before locking down an LTCI policy.

The insurer's financial condition: The insurance company or the agent you're working with should volunteer to provide an insurer's safety ratings from all the leading rating services and should provide them upon request. Decide whether you want to consider only insurers with the highest safety ratings or if you might be willing to take a policy from an insurer with a lower safety rating because of its lower cost.

It is also advisable to look at the ownership of the insurance company. In recent years some private equity funds and hedge funds have acquired insurance companies, and some advisors believe that these new owners are taking on more risk in the investment portfolios of the insurance companies in order to increase profits. The insurance companies are still regulated by state insurance commissioners who review the portfolios, establish limits on the risks that insurers can take, and requires them to maintain adequate reserves. You need to decide if the ownership of the insurer is a concern to you.

Premium increases: This is an issue with traditional LTCI policies, especially after a number of insurers imposed significant premium increases following 2008. You can review the history of premium increases for policies similar to those you are considering. The insurance agent should make them available. If not, the state insurance commissioner should have them available upon request.

Issuers of hybrid policies say they won't increase the cost of the LTC benefits under the policies, but keep in mind the hybrid policies have been available a relatively short time.

Joint policies for married couples: A married couple can usually purchase a joint policy covering the couple instead of purchasing two individual policies. The cost of a joint policy is typically less than for two individual policies. But under a joint policy there's still a maximum benefit, so it's possible that one spouse will exhaust all or most of the benefits under the policy and leave the other spouse with few or no benefits.

The long-term care insurance partnership: Most states now participate in what is called the Long-Term Care Insurance Partnership Program, a joint federal-state project that encourages people who otherwise would rely on Medicaid to pay for their LTC to instead carry private LTCI. A state and its Medicaid program can seek reimbursement of amounts paid for LTC, and this program limits the circumstances under which the states and Medicaid will attempt to recover amounts they spent on LTC from the estate, family, or exempt assets of the person who claimed the benefits.

The terms of participation in the program vary from state to state. For example, some states don't consider LTCI policies that were issued in other states. States have different formulas for the extent to which LTCI benefits will offset the amount of Medicaid LTC spending the state might seek to recover from an estate.

The Continuing-Care Alternative

An alternative to purchasing LTCI is to move into a continuing care retirement community (CCRC). A CCRC has all the types of senior living in one community, usually on one campus. There will be independent living, assisted living, memory care, skilled nursing care, and perhaps other forms of care as well. In some CCRCs you make a large deposit to enter the community, and the deposit might or might not be refundable under certain circumstances. But the deposit plus your monthly fees guarantees that you'll be admitted to whichever level of care you need and limits your monthly fees regardless of the change in care. There are several types of CCRC arrangements, but this type is known as a Type A contract CCRC.

A CCRC of this type is essentially a substitute for long-term care insurance. Your deposit buys the guarantee of care with fixed monthly fees. If you already have LTCI, the policy might pay some of the monthly fees after you need LTC. A full discussion of CCRCs is beyond the scope of this book. But if you're considering a CCRC, be sure to consider the different types of contracts available and make sure to examine the financial strength of the CCRC and any parent company.

CHAPTER 9

IRAs and 401(k)s:
Maximizing the After-Tax Value of Your Most Valuable Assets

Accumulating money in a retirement account is a straightforward process. But deciding how and when to take money out of traditional Individual Retirement Arrangements (IRAs) and 401(k)s can quickly become complicated. A consequence of this is that during the distribution process people leave a lot of money on the table for the IRS.

The tax benefits of traditional IRAs and 401(k)s are really only loans. Think of them as a mortgage on your IRA or 401(k). You receive tax benefits on the front end, when money is put into these accounts and also while investment returns compound. But eventually the mortgage must be paid when money is distributed from the accounts.

In addition, Congress is impatient to receive its mortgage payments. It wants payments to begin during the owner's lifetime. To force repayment of the loan, the government imposes required minimum distributions (RMDs) annually after the owner reaches age seventy-two. Beneficiaries who inherit the accounts must also take RMDs.

Congress says the tax advantages of an IRA are to encourage saving for the owner's retirement—but only for the owner's retirement. These aren't pots of money to be hoarded indefinitely or left for heirs. When an account is left to heirs, they should have to distribute it, and pays taxes on it. That's Congress's view.

In this chapter I assume you already have money in an IRA or 401(k) or both. You're in or nearing the retirement years, and it's time to develop a plan for taking money out of the accounts in the most tax-wise ways possible, maximizing the after-tax amount for you and your heirs. We're going to look primarily at RMDs for owners of retirement accounts. After explaining the RMD rules, I explore strategies for minimizing RMDs where possible, for optimizing after-tax RMDs during the owner's lifetime, and for maximizing the after-tax values of the retirement accounts available to heirs.

The Basic Rules and Strategies for RMDs

The rules for RMDs have changed several times, most recently in 2019 in the Setting Every Community Up for Retirement Enhancement (SECURE) Act. The SECURE Act delayed RMDs a little and simplified them a bit for IRA owners. But the Act complicated RMDs for beneficiaries who inherit IRAs from the original owners, and the IRS complicated them further with proposed regulations issued in 2022. Those complications for beneficiaries also complicate the planning for many owners of valuable IRAs and 401(k)s. I'm not going to discuss the rules for beneficiaries in detail, but most IRA beneficiaries, even beneficiaries of Roth IRAs, must take full distribution of the accounts within ten years after inheriting them. This requirement is likely intended to increase the taxes on inherited IRAs and to cause other disadvantages. Because of this, owners of IRAs may want to use some of the estate planning strategies discussed at the end of this chapter to reposition their IRAs.

The RMD rules apply to more than traditional IRAs. They also apply to traditional 401(k) plans, SEP IRAs, SIMPLE IRAs, 403(b) plans, 457(b) plans, profit sharing plans, and any other defined-contribution plans. The rules also apply to defined-benefit plans (traditional pension plans) but I won't discuss those plans in this book. I focus the discussion on traditional IRAs and occasionally note when 401(k) plans have different rules. Note that original owners of Roth IRAs don't have RMDs during their lifetimes, but beneficiaries who inherit Roth IRAs are subject to the same RMD rules as beneficiaries of traditional IRAs. Owners of Roth 401(k)s do have lifetime RMDs.

The Forced-Distribution Phase

The voluntary distribution period for IRA owners is the time after age fifty-nine and a half and before age seventy-two. Distributions before age fifty-nine and a half are potentially subject to the 10 percent early-distribution penalty, but distributions after that age avoid the penalty. Income taxes still must be paid on distributions from traditional IRAs, but there's no additional 10 percent penalty for distributions after fifty-nine and a half.

Age seventy-two is the beginning of the forced-distribution phase for all IRA owners. (Before 2020, the key age for RMDs was seventy and a half. But the SECURE Act changed the trigger age to seventy-two for everyone who turned seventy and a half after 2019.) The tax law requires distributions to begin on a regular schedule that has limited flexibility. Financial institutions are required to report to the IRS the age of each IRA owner and the value of distributions taken annually. The penalty for not taking the full required distribution is 50 percent of the amount that was required to be withdrawn but was not. (The owner can request the IRS to waive the penalty, but there is no guarantee it will be waived. As I write, there's a proposal that Congress is likely to enact at some point to reduce this penalty.)

As you will learn in this chapter, after-tax wealth is increased when an IRA owner begins planning strategies and distributions before age seventy-two.

An owner aged seventy-two or older must pay careful attention to the RMD rules, including the required beginning date, the options for calculating distributions, and the timing of annual distributions.

When RMDs Must Begin

The first RMD must be taken no later than April 1 of the year after the owner turns age seventy-two. That is known as the required beginning date (RBD). Subsequent RMDs must be taken no later than December 31 of each calendar year after the owner turned seventy-two.

Example: Max turned seventy-two in January 2022. Max's first RMD must be taken no later than April 1, 2023. (If Max had turned age 72 in December 2022, the first RMD must still be taken by April 1, 2023.) Max must take additional RMDs by each December 31, beginning December 31, 2023.

An Exception to the Rule

The RBD is different for an employer-sponsored retirement plan, such as a 401(k), when the account owner still is working for that employer. The first distribution may be delayed until April 1 of the year after the employee actually leaves the service of the employer if the employee is not a 5 percent or greater owner of the employer. Only

RMDs from that employer plan can be delayed. The person must still take RMDs after age seventy-two from any IRAs and from any retirement plans sponsored by employers other than the current employer. Once an employee leaves the service of that employer after age seventy-two, RMDs will have to be taken from accounts sponsored by that employer.

Timing the First Two RMDs

The second RMD must be taken by December 31 of the year after the year in which the owner turned age seventy-two, and an RMD must be taken by December 31 of each year after that. Recall that the first required distribution must be taken by April 1 of the year after the year in which the owner turned 72, known as the RBD. An IRA owner who waits until the RBD or near it to take the first RMD will be taking two RMDs in one year.

Example: In the example above, Max turned seventy-two in 2022, took his first RMD on March 15, 2023, and had to take another RMD by December 31, 2023. So, he'll take two RMDs in 2023.

But Max could have taken distributions any time during the year he turned seventy-two and had them count as all or part of his first RMD. An IRA owner can reduce taxes by taking the first distribution by Dec. 31 of the calendar year he or she turns seventy-two instead of waiting until April 1 of the following year.

How RMDs Are Calculated

Two numbers go into the basic RMD calculation: the account balance on Dec. 31 of the year before the RMD and the appropriate life expectancy factor. The life-expectancy factor is taken from one of the tables issued by the IRS. Once the appropriate table is located, the life-expectancy factor is found using the owner's age as of the end of the year for which the distribution will be taken. Then the account balance is divided by the life expectancy factor. The result is the RMD for the year.

The life expectancy tables are in IRS Publication 590-B, "Distributions from Individual Retirement Arrangements (IRAs)," available free from the IRS and on its website. Most retirement-account owners use "Table III–Uniform Lifetime." But "Table II–Joint Life" is used by an account owner whose sole primary beneficiary is a spouse who is more than ten years younger than the owner. And "Table I–Single Life" is for beneficiaries of inherited IRAs.

Example. Max Profits turned age seventy-two in January of 2022. His IRA balance on Dec. 31, 2021, was $350,000. Max consults Table III -Uniform Lifetime and finds his life expectancy factor at age 72 is 27.4 years. He divides $350,000 by 27.4 to calculate an RMD of $12,773.72. He also notes that the life expectancy factor for the next year will be 26.5.

It's important to use the latest life expectancy tables issued. The IRS adjusted the life expectancy factors in late 2021 (to be used in 2022 and later years) to reflect longer life expectancies. The IRS plans to update the life expectancy tables every few years, so be sure you have the latest tables.

Many brokers and other IRA custodians calculate the RMD and state the amount in each monthly statement, in the first statement of the year, or in the owner's online account.

Owners of Roth IRAs don't have to take RMDs from those IRAs, but RMDs are required by owners of traditional IRAs and 401(k)s as well as Roth 401(k)s. Beneficiaries of all inherited retirement accounts must take RMDs. The rules for those distributions are different and aren't discussed in this book.

Optimizing and Reducing RMDs

Many people find that over time RMDs increase their income taxes. That's because the life expectancy factor tables increase the percentage of the IRA to be distributed each year. The year someone turns seventy-two, 3.65 percent of the account is distributed. By age eighty-two, 5.41 percent must be distributed. Someone with assets and income in addition to the IRA might not need the full RMD to pay for living expenses, so the RMD simply increases income taxes, and that becomes more of a problem over time.

In this section, we look at some special rules that can make RMDs more efficient or less burdensome.

RMDs When You Have More than One Account

When someone owns multiple IRAs, the IRA owner has the option of aggregating the RMDs and taking the total from the IRAs in any combination he or she wants. First, the RMD is computed for each IRA. Then the owner can add the RMDs for all the IRAs into a total or aggregate RMD. Finally, the owner decides the portion of the aggregate RMD to distribute from each IRA.

The aggregate RMD can be withdrawn from the different accounts in any proportion desired by the owner. It can all be taken from one account, equal amounts can be taken from each IRA, or a different amount can be withdrawn from each account. Any pattern is acceptable if the total withdrawn by December 31 equals at least the aggregate RMD.

The balances of the following types of accounts may be aggregated when computing the RMD: traditional IRAs, Simplified Employee Pensions (SEPs), and SIMPLE IRAs.

Employer-qualified retirement plans can't be aggregated. The RMD is computed separately for each plan and each plan's RMD must be distributed from that plan.

You Can Distribute Assets

You don't have to sell any investments to make an RMD or any other type of distribution. Property can be distributed from an IRA, in what is known as an in-kind distribution. Suppose you own shares of different mutual funds in your traditional IRA. You can tell the IRA custodian to distribute shares of one or more mutual funds. The custodian transfers the shares from the IRA to a taxable account.

When you make an in-kind distribution, the amount of the distribution is the fair market value of the property on the date of the distribution. This is easy to find for publicly traded assets such as stocks, bonds, and mutual funds, but you might need an appraisal or other estimate to determine the value of other assets. Only the value on the date of the distribution counts.

That value is included in gross income, to the extent the RMD is taxable. The value on the date of the distribution is also the tax basis of the asset in your taxable account. You'll use that basis to determine the gain or loss when you eventually sell the asset.

Make Charitable Contributions from Your IRA

When you reach age seventy and a half or older, and are charitably inclined, you can avoid or reduce the tax pain of RMDs by making charitable contributions from your traditional IRA that meet the requirements for qualified charitable distributions (QCDs). With a QCD, you convert a taxable distribution into a tax-free distribution. A QCD is usually a smarter way to make charitable contributions than writing checks, even if the contribution by check is fully deductible.

When you make a charitable contribution that doesn't qualify as a QCD from your IRA, the charitable contribution is treated as a distribution and included in your gross income. It doesn't matter if the money is transferred directly from the IRA to the charity or is first distributed to you and you transfer it to the charity. (There might be a tax deduction for the non-QCD contribution if you itemize expenses on Schedule A.)

But a charitable contribution from a traditional IRA that qualifies as a QCD isn't included in your gross income. The tradeoff is that you don't receive a charitable deduction. The big bonus is that the QCD counts toward the RMD for the year, if one is required. You can take all or part of the RMD as a QCD and not have to include it in gross income. It's the only tax-free way to satisfy the RMD obligation.

You can make a QCD any time after age seventy and a half, though RMDs don't begin until age seventy-two.

By making your charitable contributions through QCDs, the money is taken out of your traditional IRA without increasing your tax bill. The non-IRA money you might have donated to charity can pay other expenses. You made your RMD for the year tax free or, if you aren't subject to RMDs yet, you reduced future RMD tax free by taking the money out of the IRA before age seventy-two.

In a year when you want to convert all or part of a traditional IRA to a Roth IRA and also have to take an RMD, you can take the RMD as a QCD so that it won't be taxable. Otherwise, you'd have to take the RMD first and include it in gross income before converting any amount to a Roth IRA.

How a Distribution Qualifies as a QCD

For a distribution to a charity to be a QCD, the traditional IRA owner must be at least age seventy and a half on the date of the transfer from the IRA to the charity. To qualify as a QCD, a charitable contribution must be made directly from the traditional IRA to a charity. The IRA owner can direct the charity to distribute the money directly to a charity or charities, or the IRA custodian can give the owner a check made out to the charity, which the owner can deliver to the charity. Some custodians give IRA owners checkbooks. The owners can take IRA distributions by writing checks. When such a check is made out to a charity, that gift is a QCD.

The Limits of QCDs

The QCDs can exceed your RMD for the year. If your RMD is $10,000, and you want to give $20,000 to charity during year, the entire $20,000 can be contributed as QCDs. But only $10,000 will count as an RMD. The other $10,000 won't be carried forward to the next year to offset its RMD. Your QCDs also can be less than your RMD for the year, in which case you must take the rest of the RMD as taxable distributions.

QCDs are limited to $100,000 each year, even if your RMD is more than $100,000. The limit is per taxpayer (not per IRA). In a married couple, each spouse has a separate $100,000 limit, but you can't share the limits or split the QCDs. Charitable contributions exceeding $100,000 in a year will be non-QCD taxable distributions and won't count toward RMDs. (Unused portions of the $100,000 limit don't carry forward to future years. The $100,000 is a use-it-or-lose-it limit.)

In general, QCDs can be made only from traditional IRAs. They can be made from a simplified employee pension (SEP) or SIMPLE IRA only when the plan hasn't received an employer contribution in the plan year that ends with or during the calendar year in which the charitable contribution is to be made. In other words, the SEP or SIMPLE IRA must be inactive.

QCDs can't be made from other employer plans, including 401(k)s. QCDs can be made from inherited traditional IRAs.

You can't receive any benefit from the charity, and you must follow the basic rules for proving charitable contributions. You must have an acknowledgement in writing from the charity regarding the amount and date of the contribution. For large donations, additional proof might be required.

Only donations from an IRA to public charities, also known as 501(c)(3) organizations, qualify as QCDs. You don't receive QCD treatment for contributions to private foundations, donor-advised funds, and other tax-exempt groups that don't qualify as public charities. A contribution from an IRA to fund a charitable gift annuity also doesn't qualify as a QCD.

The SECURE Act permits contributions to traditional IRAs after age seventy and a half, but it prohibits an individual from combining tax-deductible IRA contributions made after age seventy and a half with a QCD. Details of these rules are complicated. The key point is you shouldn't make a deductible contribution to a traditional IRA after age seventy and a half if you also plan to receive the benefits of making QCDs.

Consider a QLAC

Qualified longevity annuity contracts (QLAC) were created in regulations issued by the IRS in 2014. They're an IRS-approved way to secure a lifetime stream of income from your IRA while reducing RMDs for several years during retirement.

In a QLAC you deposit a lump sum with an insurer and receive a promise that the insurer will pay you a guaranteed lifetime stream of income in the future. You decide when the income payments will begin, within limits. Income payments can start as early as seventy-two or as late as eighty-five. The income payments are delayed for as little as two years or as many as forty-five years (but no later than to age eighty-five) after you buy the annuity.

A QLAC also reduces RMDs in years before the income payments begin. The IRA balance invested in QLACs isn't used to calculate your RMDs until income from the QLAC begins or you turn age eighty-five, whichever occurs first. The maximum QLAC investment that can be excluded from the RMD calculation is $145,000 or 25 percent of your IRA balance, whichever is less. The $145,000 limit is indexed for inflation; that amount is for 2022. The $145,000 limit is per taxpayer, not per IRA. Married couples apply the limits per person. Each spouse can invest up to $145,000 or 25 percent of his or her IRA in QLACs.

QLACs can also be purchased through participating 401(k) and similar plans in order to reduce RMDs the same way. The 25 percent limit applies to each plan, and the $145,000 limit is per person.

Estate-Planning Strategies to End the Confusion and Inconvenience of RMDs and Leave More After-Tax Wealth to Your Heirs

RMDs can cause some significant problems and planning headaches, especially for people who own traditional IRAs and 401(k)s with large balances.

One problem is lifetime income taxes. Since each year a higher percentage of the traditional IRA must be distributed under the RMD rules, the amount of the RMDs can increase significantly over time, even as the owner's spending is declining. The distributions are taxed as ordinary income at the IRA owner's highest tax rate. They also could trigger higher taxes on Social Security benefits, higher Medicare premium surtaxes, and other Stealth Taxes, as described in chapter 10. IRA owners tend to begin noticing the tax pain of RMDs in their late 70s.

For the many IRA owners who have additional sources of income and assets outside the traditional IRA, RMDs become a tax and financial problem they didn't expect at the start of retirement, and the problem becomes worse each year.

Many IRA owners don't need RMDs to pay their living expenses, according to the *RMD Options Study* conducted for Allianz Life Insurance Company. The study found that 80 percent of respondents ages sixty-five to seventy-five believe they won't need all of their RMDs to pay for daily living expenses.

The second problem is that RMDs can reduce the legacy left to heirs and loved ones. The IRA owner retains only the after-tax value of the RMD and then has to decide what to do with that amount. About 71 percent of the respondents to the Allianz survey said they'd like to use the RMDs to fund a financial product that offsets some of the taxes from the RMD. More than half of the IRA owners said they planned to leave the IRAs and a portion of their other savings as a legacy. They didn't need or want to spend the RMDs and hoped to invest them to increase the value of their estates.[1]

Complicating these concerns are the effects of the SECURE Act when beneficiaries inherit the IRAs. Many IRA owners plan to leave their IRA balances to loved ones hoping that the loved ones will be able to invest most of the money for years and then eventually use it to pay for significant needs, or perhaps for their own retirement. But, under the SECURE Act, most beneficiaries who inherit IRAs (both traditional and Roth IRAs) after 2019 must fully distribute the IRAs within ten years after inheriting them. They are no longer able to make use of the tax-deferred compounding of the IRAs (or tax-free compounding of Roth IRAs) over longer periods—in what was known as the Stretch IRA. The accelerated distribution schedule under the SECURE Act essentially eliminates the Stretch IRA and reduces the after-tax wealth that beneficiaries receive from inherited IRAs.

There are strategies that can produce two benefits for IRA owners: to reduce or eliminate lifetime RMDs, and to remove or reduce the negative effects on beneficiaries of the SECURE Act, perhaps even replicating a Stretch IRA or creating yet better results. These strategies involve repositioning the traditional IRA as something else.

The strategies also can have an additional-estate planning benefit, for the IRA owner's heirs: When an IRA (whether a traditional IRA or a Roth IRA) is inherited, the beneficiary can distribute and spend the account balance as quickly as he or she wants. An IRA owner could always prevent beneficiaries from quickly spending the inherited IRA by incurring the expense of naming a trust as beneficiary of the IRA and having a trustee manage the assets and distributions. That was expensive, and it didn't always work even before the SECURE Act. It's even less practical after the SECURE Act, because the ten-year distribution rule still applies even when a trust is the beneficiary. Also, trusts reach the highest tax bracket at a much lower income level than individuals, so naming a trust as IRA beneficiary could increase taxes on the IRA distributions.

Some of the strategies that IRA owners can use to reduce their lifetime RMDs and circumvent the ten-year rule of the SECURE Act also allow the IRA owner to place more limits on distributions by beneficiaries, if that's desired, ensuring that the IRA isn't fully distributed and taxed within a few years after it is inherited.

To minimize RMDs and avoid the effects of the SECURE Act on beneficiaries, consider using one or more of the strategies described below.

Empty or Reduce Your IRA Early

Most of us learned early that a key tax-planning principle is to defer taxes whenever you can. That was good advice in the past, but now it isn't the best advice in all situations.

Years ago I ran the numbers and concluded that many people would benefit by reducing their traditional IRAs earlier than they needed to or were required to. They should take money out of the IRA, pay the income taxes, and invest the after-tax amount in a taxable account. This strategy makes the most sense when you expect income tax rates will be higher in the future, but it can also make sense when your tax rate is likely to remain the same or even decline a little.

IRA distributions are taxed as ordinary income. If your IRA is invested to earn long-term capital gains or qualified dividends, you're converting tax-advantaged income into ordinary income. Over the long term, it might be better to have the money in a taxable account than continuing to compound in the IRA, eventually to be taxed as ordinary income.

Your heirs are also likely to be better off inheriting the taxable account. When a beneficiary inherits a traditional IRA, the distributions from the IRA are taxed to the beneficiary just as they would have been to you. The beneficiary really inherits only the after-tax amount.

But when most non-IRA assets are inherited, the heirs increase the tax basis to the current fair market value at the time of the inheritance. They can sell the assets and owe no capital gains taxes. All the appreciation during your lifetime escapes taxation, giving the heirs the benefit of the full value of the assets. It's better for loved ones to inherit taxable accounts than traditional IRAs of the same value and even of greater value, to a point.

When you combine these factors with the tax consequences of RMDs as we age, it begins to make a lot of sense for some people to take some money out of the traditional IRA early, pay the taxes, and invest the after-tax amount.

Convert Your Traditional IRA to a Roth IRA

Perhaps the most frequently used strategy is to convert all or part of a traditional IRA to a Roth IRA. A conversion eliminates future RMDs for the owner and creates tax-free income and gains for the owner and beneficiaries.

Roth IRAs don't provide up-front tax advantages. There's no deduction or exclusion from income for money contributed to a Roth IRA. But the investment returns of a Roth IRA compound free of taxes, and distributions of earnings from the account (after a five-year waiting period) are tax free. In addition, the original owner of a Roth IRA doesn't have to take RMDs during his or her lifetime, which is a major reason that owners who are concerned about rising RMDs from traditional IRAs consider converting them to Roths. Under the SECURE Act, most beneficiaries who inherit a Roth IRA must fully distribute the IRA within ten years, but those distributions are tax free.

You can convert an entire traditional IRA or any lesser amount you want to a Roth IRA. There's no limit to the number of conversions you can do in a year or a lifetime, and conversions currently aren't limited by your income or the value of the IRA.

You do pay a tax to convert a traditional IRA to a Roth IRA. The amount you convert is included in gross income as though it had been distributed to you, and it is taxed as ordinary income. When you convert a traditional IRA to a Roth IRA, you are choosing to pay taxes now instead of in the future on the amount that's converted.

Converting a traditional IRA to a Roth IRA is not the best strategy for everyone. There are several factors to consider that will help you decide whether a conversion is a good strategy.

The clearest case for converting some or all of a traditional IRA to a Roth IRA is when you anticipate that you or your heirs will face higher income tax rates in the future than today. Be sure to consider more than stated income tax rates. The effects of the Stealth Taxes, as discussed in chapter 10, must be considered.

While the difference between current and future income taxes is often the most important factor in deciding whether a conversion makes sense, it's not the only factor. In the research I've done over the years, I have found it can make sense to convert all or part of a traditional IRA even when there's no change anticipated in income tax rates.

An important factor is the rate of return earned on the investments. The higher the expected investment return, the more benefit to be gained from converting the distributions from ordinary income to tax-free income earned in a Roth IRA. A very conservative investor is less likely to benefit from a conversion.

The length of time the money will compound in the Roth IRA should also be considered. The longer the gains compound tax free in the Roth IRA after a conversion, the greater the benefit can be from paying taxes early.

But that doesn't mean an older person is automatically too old to convert an IRA, especially if the primary goal is to have the IRA inherited by younger family members. When a beneficiary inherits a traditional IRA or 401(k), he or she pays taxes on the distributions just as the original owner would have. It's only the after-tax value of the traditional IRA that is really inherited. Plus, the distributions may push the beneficiary into a higher tax bracket, especially now that the SECURE Act requires those distributions to be compacted within ten years.

When the owner converts a traditional IRA to a Roth IRA, he or she is making a gift to the beneficiaries by paying the income taxes. This isn't considered a gift under the tax code, because the owner is just paying his or her own taxes. The money used to pay the taxes is also taken out of the owner's estate, making it less likely the estate will be subject to estate taxes. These are good estate-planning reasons an older person might want to convert a traditional IRA to a Roth IRA.

Another consideration when deciding whether to convert an IRA is the source of the money to pay the income taxes on the conversion. You can take money from the traditional IRA to pay the taxes on the conversion. But that money is then included in gross income with the converted amount. A conversion is more likely to pay off when money outside the IRA is used to pay the taxes.

You can convert as much or as little of the IRA as you want. One popular strategy is to convert just enough of the traditional IRA each year to keep the conversion from pushing you into the next higher tax bracket. Employing this strategy over several years is known as serial conversions.

When determining the cost of the conversion, remember that the Medicare premium surtax is determined using adjusted gross income from two years earlier for one year. The surtax for a Medicare beneficiary in 2025 will be determined using 2023 adjusted gross income. That doesn't matter if you won't be sixty-five or older in 2025. But if you'll be a Medicare beneficiary in 2025, any amount you convert in 2023 will help determine the amount of your Medicare surtax in 2025. (Details of the Medicare premium surtax are in chapter 10.)

Triggering or increasing the Medicare premium surtax (also known as IRMAA) doesn't necessarily mean that you shouldn't convert all or part of a traditional IRA in 2023 if you'll be a Medicare beneficiary in 2025. It does mean that you should estimate how a conversion in 2023 will affect the premium surtax in 2025 and understand that's part of the cost of doing the conversion.

Roth IRA distributions are tax free under federal law, but they're not tax free in all states. Check your state's tax law before deciding to do a conversion. Also, remember that a conversion can no longer be reversed. Congress repealed the ability to reverse a conversion in the 2017 tax law.

You can see that there are multiple factors to consider before deciding to convert all or part of a traditional IRA to a Roth IRA. I don't recommend making an ad hoc decision or one using intuition or rules of thumb. Instead, use IRA-conversion-calculator software. There are many calculators available either as stand-alone software or on websites. There's one I developed that is available for purchase on my website at www.retirementwatch.com. The calculator you use should take into all the factors described above and show you the final result. Use a calculator that allows you to adjust all of the factors that I discussed here, and consider using several different calculators so you can see if they provide different results.

Don't wait until the end of the year to consider converting a traditional IRA to a Roth IRA. Early in the year, carefully analyze the factors and determine whether a conversion, and how much of a conversion, could be wise for you. Then monitor retirement account values and other factors during the year. Some taxpayers find it advantageous to convert an IRA after a market decline. They convert the assets to a Roth IRA at a lower tax cost, and the ensuing recovery in asset values is tax free.

Other taxpayers find that changes in their personal situation during the year make a conversion a good idea when it was not a good idea earlier in the year. An individual might stop working, causing his or her income and tax bracket to decline. Or a taxpayer might become eligible for a large tax deduction so the deduction offsets some or all of the converted amount.

Revisit the issue regularly, especially when there are changes in your situation or in the markets.

Reposition the Traditional IRA as Life Insurance

Instead of converting a traditional IRA to a Roth IRA, you can reposition the traditional IRA as a permanent life insurance policy. The basic steps are that you take distributions from the traditional IRA, pay the income taxes, and deposit the after-tax amount in a permanent life insurance policy. There are several possible life insurance strategies that should be considered by someone who has sufficient income and assets outside the IRA to provide a secure retirement and whose primary plan for the traditional IRA is to leave it to heirs.

The life insurance payout received by the beneficiaries is income-tax free. Remember that when a traditional IRA or 401(k) is inherited, the beneficiaries pay income taxes on the distributions. They really inherit only the after-tax amount.

Another potential advantage is that the amount your loved ones will inherit with life insurance doesn't fluctuate with the markets the way an IRA balance can. The life insurance benefit is fixed by contract and may increase over time with some types of life insurance.

The benefit established with the life insurance policy is also likely to be more than the balance of the traditional IRA, and it almost certainly will be more than the after-tax value of the IRA. Details will vary with your age, health, and the type of permanent life insurance policy purchased.

The policy owner might have lifetime tax-free access to part of the policy's value, via loans from the insurer using the cash value of the policy as collateral. The loans won't have to be repaid, but outstanding loan balances will reduce the final life insurance benefit. The loans may be interest free or have a very low interest rate, depending on the life insurance policy.

Here's one example, proposed by David and Todd Phillips of Estate Planning Specialists, of how to enhance your IRA legacy using life insurance.

Suppose you are sixty-four years old and in good health and you have a $500,000 traditional IRA. You are in the 28 percent effective tax bracket. You roll over the IRA to an IRA-type account with a life insurance company. Each year for the next five years you transfer $105,732 from the account to pay the premiums on a universal life policy. These will be taxable distributions. You can pay the taxes from other sources or take a loan from the insurance policy each year to pay the taxes. The policy benefit is more than $1.1 million, payable to the beneficiaries you name. (Keep in mind that the details vary based on interest rates, the age and health of the insured, and other factors.)

After five years the policy is paid up, and the IRA-type account is empty. You won't have to take required minimum distributions from an IRA in the future. You converted the IRA into life insurance with no out-of-pocket cost if you used policy loans to pay the income taxes. The loans used to pay the taxes eventually are subtracted from the policy benefit.

In another strategy, you reposition the IRA as a family dynasty trust fund with a permanent life insurance policy.

Suppose you are married, and you're both seventy-one and in good health. You have a $1 million traditional IRA and plan to leave most of the IRA to your children and grandchildren.

You set up a family dynasty trust that benefits your grandchildren, your children or both. You take annual RMDs from the IRA and transfer the after-tax amount to the trust. The trust buys a joint-life-and-survivor life insurance policy covering both you and your spouse with the benefit payable to the trust when the second spouse dies. (A joint-life-and-survivor policy usually maximizes the permanent life insurance benefit received per premium dollar.) The trust uses the annual gifts to pay premiums on the policy. The policy should have a benefit of around $1.4 million.

After both spouses pass away, the life insurance benefit is paid to the trust, which invests and distributes the money according to the terms you set in the trust agreement. It can be paid out to the grandchildren over years, pay for specific needs, held until they reach certain ages, or whatever other distribution you want.[2]

Remember that the insurance benefit is tax-free to the trust. Instead of the grandchildren inheriting the after-tax value of a $1 million traditional IRA (or whatever the value has changed to when it is inherited), the grandchildren's trust receives almost $1.4 million tax free. In addition, having the benefit paid to the trust instead of the individual grandchildren substantially reduces the risk that the money will be poorly invested or spent rapidly or frivolously.

These are just two examples of how an IRA can be converted into a tax-free life insurance benefit. You can talk to an estate planner and a life insurance broker to determine good strategies for you to consider.

From IRA to Charitable Remainder Trust

Another strategy to reduce RMDs (or replace the Stretch IRA) is the charitable remainder trust (CRT).

There are many possible variations of the CRT. For example, you can have the CRT pay lifetime income to your children. After they pass away, the remaining trust assets will be paid to one or more charities you named (or you can allow the CRT beneficiaries to name the charities). After creating the CRT, you name the CRT as the beneficiary of your IRA.

Immediately after you pass away, the IRA assets are distributed to the CRT trustee. There are no income taxes at this point, because the charitable trust is tax exempt. The trustee invests the CRT assets. The trust agreement determines the amount of the distributions, within guidelines set by the tax law. Distributions are spread over the beneficiaries' lifetimes, preventing the beneficiaries from spending them rapidly and wastefully. The CRT protects the assets from creditors of the beneficiaries to the extent the assets haven't been distributed.

The CRT creates results very similar to the Stretch IRA that was allowed before the SECURE Act.

Another variation is that the CRT provides income during your lifetime. You distribute the balance of the traditional IRA and transfer the after-tax proceeds to a CRT that pays income to you (or you and your spouse) for life. You'll have to include the distribution in gross income. But you're also likely to receive a charitable contribution deduction that offsets much of the income. Then, the CRT begins to pay you income for life. The income payments can begin right away, or you can set a future point at which they begin.

Convert Your IRA to Guaranteed Lifetime Income with a Charitable Gift Annuity

CRTs are very flexible, but there are a lot of details involved in creating a CRT. You'll need to work with an experienced estate planner to determine the best structure for you. If you want to reduce RMDs and benefit a charity, consider making use of a related strategy: converting all or part of your traditional IRA into a charitable gift annuity (CGA).

A CGA is much like a commercial annuity, as discussed in chapter 5. The difference is the CGA is likely to make lower income payments. The dollar amount difference between CGA payments and those of a commercial annuity is a gift from you to the charity.

The CGA is simpler than the CRT. You don't have to draft a trust agreement or consider different terms. Effectively, your IRA buys an annuity from a charity. The CGA is also a good option when the assets in the IRA aren't valuable enough to justify the cost of creating and administering a CRT. If you're interested in this strategy, contact charities you want to help and ask if they offer charitable gift annuities.

Maximize the After-Tax Value of Your Retirement Accounts

IRA and 401(k) accounts are likely among your most valuable assets. Many people manage these accounts on cruise control. They miss opportunities to increase the after-tax value of the accounts and to maximize their families' after-tax wealth. It's important to consider the long-term consequences of different strategies and to integrate IRAs and 401(k)s in estate plans. People who fail to consider all their options leave money on the table for the IRS to scoop up in extra taxes—something that won't be apparent until later in retirement.

CHAPTER 10

The Five Big Retirement Tax Ambushes and How to Avoid Them

Taxes are a more significant obstacle to maintaining financial independence and security in retirement than most people realize. Many people believe their taxes will be lower in retirement. They've heard about various tax breaks for seniors and think that you're likely to pay a lower income tax rate in retirement. These ideas about taxes in retirement might have been accurate at one time, but no longer.

For most retirees, taxes are one of their top three expenses each year—when all types of taxes are considered. There aren't many special tax breaks available to those ages sixty-five and older, and the qualifications for those tax breaks are narrow. Elected officials know that most of the income and wealth in the country is controlled by people in that age group. Governments can't afford to give many tax breaks to them.

When "taxes" are mentioned, many people think only about income taxes. But there are many other types of taxes, including real

estate and personal property taxes imposed by state and local governments. Many of these taxes are likely to rise during retirement, even
when your income doesn't increase.

In this chapter I focus on federal income taxes, which are the ones
you're most likely to have some control over.

Retirees are often surprised by what some advisors call the retirement tax attack or the retirement tax torpedo. The federal income tax
code and many state tax codes contain tax traps for retirees. These are
tax rules that increase income taxes on certain individuals. Congress
and state legislatures don't want to increase overall tax rates, so, they
insert provisions in the tax code that take away tax breaks, cause more
income to be taxed, or impose additional taxes on people in certain
circumstances. These laws indirectly raise the effective tax rates of
certain individuals without raising the overall rates in the tax tables.

I call them the Stealth Taxes. These tax provisions can suddenly
and surprisingly reduce after-tax income and wealth. Many people
don't know about these taxes until they fall into the traps. Some of
the Stealth Taxes specifically target older taxpayers, while others just
happen to affect retirees more than other taxpayers.

By being proactive, you may be able to avoid or reduce some of
the Stealth Taxes. Because of the Stealth Taxes, retirees should take
a longer-term view than other taxpayers when planning with respect
to their taxes. They also need to consider tax planning and management all year long, in order to reduce the financial risks of retirement
and increase the family's after-tax income and wealth.

In this chapter, I discuss the key Stealth Taxes, explaining how
each tax works and the planning actions retirees and pre-retirees
should consider in response. I first discuss the three biggest Stealth
Taxes for retirees and strategies to avoid or reduce them. After that,
I review two additional Stealth Taxes you need to be aware of and
that are discussed in more detail in other chapters.

The Income Tax on Social Security Benefits

Social Security benefits used to be tax free for everyone. But in its 1983 reforms, Congress decided that over time Social Security benefits should be taxed similarly to private pension benefits. That means that after-tax contributions made by the beneficiary would be tax free but other benefits would be taxed as they are received. Congress also decided that lower-income beneficiaries still should receive their benefits free of federal income taxes, but other beneficiaries should not.

The result is many Social Security beneficiaries must include part of their benefits in gross income and pay income taxes on them. The value of benefits to be included in gross income is determined by a complicated formula.

In 1993, Congress decided that higher-income beneficiaries should pay even more taxes on their Social Security benefits, and the formula was made more complicated. The income taxes generated by the 1983 reforms are paid to the Social Security program. The income taxes generated by the 1993 changes are paid to the Medicare Hospital Insurance Trust Fund.

A key feature of the tax on Social Security benefits is that, unlike many other provisions of the tax code, the income levels at which Social Security benefits are included in gross income aren't indexed for inflation. They are locked in at the levels enacted in 1983 and 1993. As inflation increases nominal incomes, the percentage of Social Security beneficiaries paying income taxes on their benefits increases. The percentage went from 0 percent before the changes to 26 percent in 1998 and 49 percent in 2014. The Social Security Administration has estimated that close to 60 percent of beneficiaries pay income taxes on their benefits now. If taxes on benefits aren't indexed for inflation, it won't be long before about 80 percent of beneficiaries pay income taxes on their benefits.[1]

State income taxes on Social Security benefits are a different story. Seven states don't have an income tax (Alaska, Florida, Nevada, South Dakota, Texas, Washington, and Wyoming). Utah follows the federal formula for taxing Social Security benefits. Twelve states tax all or part of Social Security benefits but use formulas that differ from the federal formula (Colorado, Connecticut, Kansas, Minnesota, Missouri, Montana, Nebraska, New Mexico, North Dakota, Rhode Island, Vermont, and West Virginia). The remaining thirty states and the District of Columbia exempt Social Security benefits from income taxes.

Since the federal formula for taxing Social Security benefits is complicated, most people should use tax return preparation software or a professional tax preparer when your benefits are taxable. But I'll summarize the formula so you can see how it works and understand how to reduce the tax on your benefits.

You start with something called "provisional income." That's the gross income reported on your income tax return other than Social Security benefits plus one-half of your Social Security benefits. If the total doesn't exceed the base amount, none of the Social Security benefits are taxable. The base amounts are $32,000 for a married couple filing jointly and $25,000 for single taxpayers and heads of households.

If provisional income exceeds the base amount, then some portion of the Social Security benefits probably will be taxable. There are two tiers of taxable benefits. Up to 50 percent of benefits are included in gross income in the lower tier. The lower tier for single individuals applies when modified adjusted gross income (MAGI) is $25,000 to $34,000. (The lower tier for married couples filing jointly is when MAGI is $32,000 to $44,000.) In the second tier, up to 85 percent of benefits are included in gross income. The second tier is when MAGI exceeds the first-tier ceiling, $34,000 for single taxpayers and $44,000 for married taxpayers filing jointly.

Your MAGI is your gross income plus one-half of your Social Security benefits, any tax-exempt interest, and certain less commonly used exclusions such as foreign earned income and housing allowances, adoption benefits, and a few others. You can still subtract any deductions for adjusted gross income for which you qualify, such as health savings account contributions, one-half of self-employment taxes, and other deductions that are listed on Schedule 1 that accompanies Form 1040.

When MAGI exceeds the floor of the first tier, the amount of Social Security benefits equal to 50 percent of the amount of MAGI exceeding the tier floor are included in gross income, up to a maximum of 50 percent of the total benefits. In the second tier, Social Security benefits equal to 85 percent of the amount of MAGI exceeding the tier floor are included in gross income, up to a maximum of 85 percent of the total benefits.

You can see why I recommend that most people use tax preparation software or a tax return preparer to help calculate the amount of Social Security benefits included in gross income. But if you want to figure the tax yourself, the IRS has a detailed worksheet on its web site and in Publication 915, "Social Security and Equivalent Railroad Retirement Benefits."

Because of this tax, Social Security beneficiaries can face some of the highest marginal tax rates among all taxpayers. The marginal tax rate is the tax rate on your last dollar of income. For most taxpayers, the marginal tax rate is the same as the rate for their tax bracket. But when you face the tax on Social Security benefits and other Stealth Taxes, an additional dollar of income can cause more than one dollar to be included in gross income or can trigger taxes other than regular income taxes.

In the first tier of the Social Security benefits tax, an additional dollar of income can cause fifty cents of Social Security benefits to be added to gross income. So, you're taxed on $1.50 of income for each additional dollar of income you earn. In the second tier, you're taxed on $1.85 of income for each additional dollar earned. If someone in the 12 percent tax bracket earns an additional dollar of income, income taxes increase by twelve cents. But for someone receiving Social Security benefits who falls into the first tier of taxes on the benefits, that additional dollar of income could result in 18 cents of additional taxes.

For married couples the inclusion of Social Security benefits in gross income is determined using the joint income of the couple. It doesn't matter if one spouse is receiving benefits and the other is not, even when the spouse not receiving benefits earned most of the couple's income for the year. The benefits will be taxed on the couple's joint tax bracket. Choosing the married filing separately status just makes things worse, because the base amount for taxing Social Security benefits is $0 for those taxpayers.

You can see that reducing MAGI and adjusted gross income (AGI) is the key to lowering taxes on Social Security benefits. Reducing those types of income also is the key to reducing the other Stealth Taxes. I'll review the other Stealth Taxes and then discuss strategies for reducing MAGI and AGI.

The Medicare Premium Surtax

Every Medicare beneficiary pays a base premium for Part B of Medicare, and those who take out policies in the Part D prescription drug program pay the insurance company's standard premium for their policies. (See chapter 7 for details about Medicare.) But as income rises, higher premiums are charged for both Part B and Part D Medicare coverage. The additional premiums are the Income-Related Monthly Adjustment Amount (IRMAA), also known as the Medicare

Chart 10.1 Who Paid Higher Medicare Premiums in 2022?

2020 MAGI Individual	2020 MAGI Married Joint	Part B Monthly Premium	Part D Monthly Surtax	Total Monthly Surtaxes
91,000.00	182,000.00	$170.10	$0.00	$0.00
114,000.00	228,000.00	$238.10	$12.40	$80.40
142,000.00	284,000.00	$340.20	$32.10	$202.20
170,000.00	340,000.00	$442.30	$51.70	$323.90
≤500000	≤750000	$544.30	$71.30	$445.50
> $500,000	> $750,000	$578.30	$77.90	$486.10

The Medicare premium surtax (IRMAA) imposed at different levels of Adjusted Gross Income for both Part B and Part D of Medicare in 2022

premium surtax. As with the other Stealth Taxes, it is based on MAGI and increase as MAGI rises.

The base monthly Medicare Part B premium in 2022 was $170.10. Table 12-1 shows how the premium increases as income increases, because of IRMAA. There are six premium levels, and the premium topped out at $578.30 when income exceeded $500,000 for individuals and $750,000 for married couples. Those numbers are per beneficiary. A married couple in which both spouses are Medicare beneficiaries will pay that amount twice over. Both the Medicare base premium and the income levels at which the Medicare premium surtax are paid are indexed for inflation each year, so the numbers in the table change each year.

The Medicare premium surtax was created by the Medicare Modernization Act of 2003 and first imposed in 2007 to add means-testing to Medicare by charging higher-income beneficiaries higher premiums for Parts B and D of the program. The basic Part B premium is supposed to pay for 25 percent of expected costs for the program for the year. Under the premium surtax, higher-income beneficiaries pay higher percentages of the estimated program costs as their incomes increase. A 2015 law applied the surtax to lower income levels beginning in 2018.

You can have premiums for both Parts B and D withheld from your Social Security benefits. If you elect that, the IRMAA amounts will be automatically withheld, along with the base amounts. Otherwise, you'll be billed monthly for the Part B premiums by Medicare, and the insurance company will bill you for Part D premiums.

IRMAA is imposed with a two-year lag. Your MAGI from 2021 income tax return will determine your IRMAA, if any, for 2023. The Social Security Administration (SSA) received your 2021 income tax data from the IRS in 2022 after your 2021 tax return was filed. In late 2022, the SSA sent each Medicare beneficiary a letter stating what the surtax will be in 2023.

That means that if you sign up for Medicare for the first time at age sixty-five, your modified adjusted gross income from age sixty-three is used to calculate your premium surtax for the first year.

Fortunately, you can request a reduction or elimination of the surtax if "a life-changing event" has made this year's income lower than your income two years ago.

If you just retired and therefore experienced a decline in income, you can file Form SSA-44 with the Social Security Administration and report the "work stoppage." On the form, you estimate the MAGI for the current year and provide documentation of the life-changing event and the lower income. You may also need to do this for your second year of retirement.

Other life-changing events that qualify for a change in the surtax are marriage, divorce, annulment, death of a spouse, work reduction, loss of income-producing property, loss of a pension, and an employer settlement payment due to the employer's bankruptcy received in the earlier year.

If you want to appeal the surtax and your life-changing event doesn't fit into one of those categories, consider filing a Request for Reconsideration on Form SSA-561-U2, where you state why you believe the MAGI from two years ago shouldn't be used to determine the current year's Medicare premium surtax and wait for SSA to reply.

One-time increases in income during the earlier year don't qualify you for an adjustment. Your MAGI two years earlier might have increased because you converted part of a traditional IRA to a Roth IRA. Or there might have been a taxable sale of a home, other real estate, or an investment with a substantial capital gain. You might have received a significant bonus at work or some other large one-time payment. Your surtax won't be adjusted for any of these events; you'll still owe the higher surtax this year for the jump in income two years ago. But if your income declines to normal levels in the following years, the surtax should decline or disappear.

Also, keep in mind that the "hold harmless" rule for Social Security benefits doesn't apply to the surtax. Under the hold harmless rule, when a beneficiary has Medicare Part B premiums deducted from Social Security benefits, any increase in Medicare premiums can't cause a reduction in the net Social Security benefits received. The dollar amount increase in premiums can't be more than the dollar amount increase in benefits for that year. The hold harmless rule doesn't apply to the surtax. It can, however, cause a reduction in your net Social Security benefits.

The 3.8 Percent Tax on Investment Income

The net investment income tax (NIIT) was created in the Affordable Care Act of 2008 and probably is the least-known of the Stealth Taxes. It's also the one most likely to surprise retirees. The NIIT was labeled a Medicare surtax when it was enacted, but the proceeds go into general revenues, not the Medicare trust fund.

The NIIT is a 3.8 percent tax on excess unearned, or investment, income. It is imposed on single taxpayers with a MAGI exceeding $200,000 and married couples filing jointly with MAGIs above $250,000. The income thresholds aren't indexed for inflation, so more people will owe the tax over the years. Your MAGI for this tax is your regular adjusted gross income (AGI) plus any foreign earned income that qualified for the exclusion from gross income.

Unearned income includes interest, dividends, capital gains, annuity distributions (taxable distributions only and only when not from a qualified retirement plan), royalties, and passive real estate rental income. Income from a trade or business is included as unearned income if the business is a passive activity for you.

The tax doesn't apply to tax-exempt interest, Veterans Administration benefits, or gains from the sale of a principal residence that is excluded from gross income. Distributions from IRAs, 401(k)s, and other qualified retirement plans also don't count as investment income for NIIT.

After computing total investment income for the year, net investment income is determined by subtracting any investment-related expenses. The NIIT is imposed on the lesser of net investment income and the amount of AGI above the threshold.

Suppose Max and Rosie have a net investment income of $30,000 and a MAGI of $270,000. The excess of MAGI over the threshold is $20,000. That's lower than their net investment income of $30,000, so they pay the 3.8 percent tax on $20,000. Multiplying $20,000 by 3.8 percent results in an NIIT of $760.

But suppose instead that the Profits' MAGI is $290,000 and their net investment income is still $30,000. In that case, the NIIT is lower than the difference between their MAGI and the threshold, so the tax would be computed on the net investment income. That tax would be 3.8 percent of $30,000, or $1,140.

Capital gains and qualified dividends are included in net investment income, so the NIIT effectively increases the maximum tax rate on those sources of income.

One trick to this tax is that all sources of income increase your MAGI and potentially trigger the tax, but only the "unearned" income is subject to the tax.

For example, you might take an additional IRA distribution to pay medical expenses. IRA distributions aren't subject to the surtax. But the distribution will increase your MAGI and could push you from an income level that is exempt from the surtax into one that forces you to pay the surtax on your unearned income.

How to Reduce MAGI and Beat the Biggest Stealth Taxes

The three biggest Stealth Taxes are triggered by MAGI. Those Stealth Taxes are the inclusion of Social Security benefits in gross income, the Medicare premium surtax, and the net investment income tax (NIIT). In this section, I discuss strategies to reduce MAGI and therefore reduces those Stealth Taxes, as well as your regular income taxes.

You first need to determine where your MAGI is in relation to the trigger points for these taxes or for higher levels of these taxes. The unfortunate fact is that if your MAGI is well above the trigger levels, there probably isn't much you can do to avoid or reduce the taxes. But if your MAGI is near the threshold for triggering the surtax or the next higher level of the tax, it can be worth your while to take steps during the year to reduce or eliminate the surtax, or at least to avoid increasing your MAGI and thus triggering or increasing one or more of the Stealth Taxes.

Your MAGI is computed starting with your adjusted gross income (AGI), which is on line 11 of the front page of the 2022 Form 1040. To arrive at the MAGI, the AGI is increased by any tax-exempt interest income, EE savings bond interest used for education expenses, and excluded foreign earned income you received. The definition of MAGI is a little different for some Stealth Taxes than for others. For example, tax-exempt interest isn't added back when computing MAGI for the NIIT.

MAGI isn't affected by itemized deductions, such as mortgage interest, state and local taxes and charitable contributions. Instead, you reduce MAGI by reducing gross income and by increasing the special deductions from AGI that are reported on Schedule 1 of Form 1040. Frankly, few retirees qualify for the deductions from AGI unless they're self-employed. For most people the best approach is to focus on reducing gross income.

Many retirees inadvertently trigger or increase one or more Stealth Taxes during the year by taking an action when there were alternatives that wouldn't have triggered or increased the taxes. For example, taking an additional distribution from a traditional IRA to pay for an expense will increase your MAGI, while taking a distribution from a Roth IRA or health savings account won't.

There are a few strategies you need to consider to reduce MAGI and the Stealth Taxes.

Use Tax Diversification

Tax diversification allows you to manage your tax bracket by planning and controlling cash flow from different sources during retirement. Different types of retirement and investment accounts are treated differently under the tax code. To achieve tax diversification, spread your retirement nest egg among the different types of accounts.

The primary kind of tax-deferred accounts are traditional IRAs, 401(k)s, tax-deferred annuities, and employer pensions. Taxable accounts include the regular investment accounts at brokers and mutual funds. Finally, there are tax-free accounts, primarily Roth IRAs and health savings accounts (HSAs). The cash-value account of permanent life insurance can also be considered a tax-free account.

Once your assets are spread among these different accounts, you will often be able to determine what your MAGI (and thus your tax rate) will be each year by managing how money is taken from the different accounts.

Let's take a look at the hypothetical case of Max and Rosie.

Max and Rosie anticipate receiving $60,000 of Social Security benefits. They also estimate taking $45,000 of RMDs from traditional IRAs and realizing $15,000 of long-term capital gains from their taxable accounts.

Offsetting the income is the $24,000 standard deduction for a married couple filing jointly, plus an additional $2,500 deduction for being sixty-five or older ($1,250 per spouse). That gives them a standard deduction of $26,500. Their total tax bill would be $7,461. (These numbers vary from year to year because of inflation indexing, so they aren't precise for the current year.)

Suppose this $120,000 of income doesn't meet Max and Rosie's spending plans for the year. They need an additional $5,000 of cash.

If they take that $5,000 from a traditional IRA, you might think that since they are in the 12 percent tax bracket, they'll owe $600 of additional taxes. That's not the case, because of the Stealth Taxes.

Max and Rosie are in the income range where each additional dollar of income increases the amount of their Social Security benefits that are taxed. In their case, another $4,250 of Social Security benefits are taxable at 12 percent if they take the $5,000 from a traditional IRA. Also, the additional IRA distribution plus including more Social Security benefits in gross income pushes some of their long-term capital gains out of the 0 percent bracket to the 15 percent tax bracket. When it's all added up, Max and Rosie owe an additional $2,497.50 of federal taxes because of the $5,000 IRA distribution.

If the Profits have a Roth IRA or health savings account, it makes a lot more sense for them to take that $5,000 from one of those accounts, because those distributions will be tax free. They won't be included in gross income or MAGI and won't trigger or increase any Stealth Taxes.

Other options Max and Rosie could consider would be to sell some investments from a taxable account and recognize long-term capital gains instead of incurring ordinary income from a traditional IRA distribution. Even better, if some of the investments in the taxable account are below their purchase price, they could sell them at a loss. The loss wouldn't increase their gross income and might reduce it if they can deduct it against capital gains or other income.

Use Tax-Wise Asset Location

In addition to establishing the different types of accounts and having your funds spread among the accounts, try to hold each asset in the most tax-efficient account for that particular asset, to the extent that is practical. The priority is choosing the right asset allocation for you. Then, to the extent you can, based on how much money you have in each of the different accounts, hold each investment in the type of account that is optimal for it, with respect to taxability.

The general rules for optimum asset location are simple, but there are important exceptions that can enhance your after-tax returns.

The first general rule is that investments that have their own tax advantages should be held in taxable accounts. Bonds that generate tax-free interest, for example, should be in taxable accounts. Qualified dividends, which are dividends paid on most stocks of U.S.-based companies, have the tax advantage of a maximum 20 percent tax rate, so it is best to hold them in taxable accounts. Master limited partnerships are also usually best held in taxable accounts, because they have their own tax benefits, and their earnings might be taxable when they're held in IRAs.

Stocks, exchange-traded funds, and mutual funds should usually be held in taxable accounts, when possible, because they earn long-term capital gains taxed at the maximum 20 percent rate when held for more than one year. (Many taxpayers pay less than the 20 percent rate on long-term capital gains.) In addition, when these assets are held in taxable accounts, losses can be deducted against other capital gains, and up to $3,000 of capital losses that exceed capital gains for the year can be deducted against other types of income.

Tax-deferred accounts should hold investments that generate ordinary income, such as ordinary interest and nonqualified dividends. The tax-deferred account lets the income compound to a higher amount before it is taxed than if the assets were held in taxable accounts. These assets include most types of bonds, CDs, and the like. Investments that generate short-term capital gains also should be considered for tax-deferred accounts.

When assets that can generate qualified dividends or long-term capital gains are held in a tax-deferred account, a tax-advantaged investment return is effectively converted into ordinary income and taxed at higher rates. That's because all distributions from tax-deferred accounts are taxed as ordinary income, even if they would be tax-favored long-term capital gains or preferred dividends in a taxable account. Also, losses on stocks and other capital investments can't be deducted when they're owned in a tax-deferred account.

The optimum investments for tax-free accounts such as Roth IRAs are those with the highest returns. Distributions from the accounts are tax free and the earnings compound tax free within the account. You maximize tax-free income by having the highest-returning investments in the tax-free account.

Let's look at some exceptions to these general rules.

While the general rule is to hold stocks and stock funds in taxable accounts because they already have favorable tax treatment, that's not always the optimum choice.

These assets are best held in taxable accounts when you will hold them for more than one year, so that your gains are long-term capital gains. When you are likely to sell and recognize gains before holding the asset for more than one year, the gains will be taxed as ordinary income anyway. It is then better to shelter them in a tax-deferred account so they compound to a higher value before being distributed and taxed as ordinary income. In a taxable account, the short-term gains would be taxed each year, so they would compound to a lower amount before being taxed, and they would increase your MAGI each year.

Another exception to the general rule is that some mutual funds distribute a significant portion of their gains each year. Such funds are best held in tax-deferred accounts. The best fund choices for taxable accounts are index funds, most ETFs, and mutual funds with low turnover ratios.

Some researchers conclude that stocks and mutual funds are optimum for taxable accounts only if you hold them for years and their returns compound at a high rate. Tax-deferred and tax-free accounts are the optimum places to hold assets that involve more frequent buying and selling.

My research over the years has found that you're better off in the long term by holding the higher-returning assets—assets whose pre-tax returns, from stocks or other investments, are significantly higher than returns from other investments—in a tax-deferred account. The compounding of the higher returns is more important over the long term than the tax benefit of the long-term capital gains rate of the taxable account. My research indicates that the tipping point is when stock returns exceed returns of your other investments by more than four percentage points. At that point, after-tax returns often are optimized by having the stock returns compound in a tax-deferred account.

It's also important to keep in mind that the ordinary income tax rate at the time when assets are put in a tax-deferred account might not be the same as when returns are distributed from the tax-deferred account. Someone who is in the highest income tax bracket during the working years might be in a lower tax bracket after retiring. When you expect to be in a lower tax bracket in retirement, the optimum strategy can be to put higher-returning assets in tax-deferred accounts during the accumulation years so the gains won't be taxed while you're subject to the higher tax rate. The returns will be taxed at the lower rate when they're distributed during your retirement years.

But with those caveats, your highest-earning investments should generally be held in tax-free accounts, such as Roth IRAs, whenever possible, as discussed above.

Of course, the overall asset allocation is the dominant consideration. Once that decision is made, you should try, to the extent possible, to hold the investments in accounts that maximize after-tax returns. You may not be able to allocate assets exactly in the optimum way, but you should strive to get as close as possible.

Manage Taxable Investment Accounts

Transactions in your taxable investment accounts affect gross income and MAGI.

Taking capital gains by selling investments in taxable accounts increases your income and therefore the amount of your benefits that are taxed. So before selling appreciated investments, consider how the sale might affect MAGI. You might want to delay taking some gains until next year or recognize some losses in your portfolio to offset the gains.

On the other hand, if you already triggered the maximum Stealth Taxes or were pushed into the lower level of the next higher bracket, you might want to take some additional gains that you were likely to take within the next year anyway. Moving the income into this year could decrease your MAGI and thus both your income and Stealth Taxes next year.

Mutual funds can make significant year-end distributions that increase your taxable benefits. Some people find it helpful to switch from actively managed funds to index funds or to actively managed funds that have historically low distributions to avoid large taxable distributions near the end of the year. Other investors contact the funds for estimates of their late-year distributions and plan to take some capital losses or make other adjustments in years when fund distributions will be high.

The Widow's Penalty Tax

The widow's penalty tax isn't well known yet it is one of the most onerous of the retirement Stealth Taxes. Since few people are aware of it, few retirement plans defend against the widow's penalty. The tax pitfalls of what I call the solo years (the period after one spouse passes away) are so significant that I devote a separate chapter to them. Details about the widow's penalty tax are discussed in chapter 13, along with other aspects of the solo years.

RMDs and the SECURE Act

The last Stealth Tax is imposed on large traditional IRAs and 401(k)s. There are two versions of this Stealth Tax. The first is the higher income taxes to which the owners of these accounts are subject to over time because of required minimum distributions (RMDs). The second is the higher taxes beneficiaries who inherit these accounts might pay because of the Setting Every Community Up for Retirement Enhancement (SECURE) Act that was enacted in 2019. The consequences of RMDs and how to avoid them are discussed in chapter 9.

CHAPTER 11

Ensure Your Legacy:
Estate Planning Is Much More than Tax Reduction

An estate plan needs to be part of your retirement planning. Don't fall into the trap of thinking estate planning is only for the very wealthy. That became a widespread belief after the 2001 tax law increased the lifetime estate and gift tax exemption. It became an even more widespread belief after the 2017 tax law doubled the exemption. In 2022, the lifetime exemption stood at $12.06 million, or $24.12 million for a married couple. Only a small percentage of estates pay federal estate and gift taxes.

That doesn't mean you can skip the estate plan.

Estate planning is much more than tax reduction and always has been. Before 2001, estate taxes were the focus of estate planning for even middle-class people, because without planning, the tax would take a meaningful portion of even modest estates. Since most estates are now exempt from federal estate and gift taxes, people can focus on the key issues of estate planning that were side issues for many years because of worries about taxes. These nontax issues should have been the focus of estate planning all along, and now they should even capture the attention of families with very modest wealth.

A complete estate plan provides benefits during your lifetime, ensuring that you're taken care of during your later years and that your wealth is protected during your lifetime. The estate plan also transfers the wealth to whomever you want in the way you want, with minimal cost, delay, controversy, and conflict. Estate planning should first focus on taking care of you and your assets during your lifetime. The secondary issues are how much to give, when to give, and in what form to give your property to others.

I'm not going to say much in this chapter about the federal estate and gift tax, because it now applies to so few estates. But be aware that unless Congress makes a change, the 2017 tax law will expire after 2025. The lifetime estate and gift tax exemption will be cut in half for 2026, and other changes will take effect automatically. Until then, focus on the important non-tax issues of estate planning that apply to everyone.

The Key Documents

Certain documents are essential for every estate plan, and the complete plan includes more than just a will. As I like to say, a will is not an estate plan. While someone who has a very valuable or complicated estate, or a complicated family, might have more estate planning documents than others, there are certain documents that everyone, whether he is Elon Musk or the sub-millionaire next door, should have ready. Estate plans that fail often do so because one or more of these documents was absent or wasn't given enough attention. Take care that these documents are in your estate plan and meet your needs.

The essential documents are:

<u>Will</u>: Everyone should have a written will, even those who have a living trust or have taken other actions to avoid probate and transfer their assets.

<u>Revocable living trust</u>: In most states, a living trust is a good way to avoid the cost and delay of probate. It can be a good way to smooth the transition of management and ownership of most assets during your lifetime and afterward, and it works in every state.

<u>Power of attorney</u>: A power of attorney ensures that someone is authorized to manage your assets anytime you aren't able to. Having one is important both to preserving your estate and to reducing problems for your loved ones.

<u>Medical directive:</u> This can be one document or several, depending on the state you live in and the attorney you use. Other names for this document are living will, advance medical directive, and medical power of attorney. In general, a medical directive ensures that one or more people is authorized to make medical decisions when you aren't able to and that the decisions are likely to be in line with your wishes.

<u>Letter of instructions and inventory</u>: This package of documents helps those who are administering your estate to do so efficiently and implement your wishes. It also helps heirs who are bequeathed assets from your estate.

Let's discuss each of these documents in detail.

The Will

A will is a written statement of your instructions and intentions regarding your estate.

The maker of the will is the testator. The person who oversees administration of the estate and compliance with the terms of the will and state law is known as the executor, administrator, or personal representative (depending on the state). When you leave property to someone in your will, that's known as a bequest, and the person receiving the property is a beneficiary.

Probate is the process under which your will and estate are administrated and settled. Some states have separate probate courts, while in others a family court, or the regular district or circuit court handles probate.

Dying without a will is called dying intestate. When someone dies intestate, state law determines how the estate is distributed, and the court appoints someone to act as executor.

<u>More than property.</u> The main purpose of a will is to direct how you want your property distributed, but it should include other directions.

You can appoint one or more people to serve as executor. Often the court accepts the appointment in the will, but it might not be required to. If you have minor children or dependents, you can designate their guardian or guardians. If you don't, state law will determine who becomes responsible for them. You also can include any desires you have concerning the funeral, memorial service, and treatment of your body. In some states, these directions are binding, but in others they are only suggestions and preferences.

Other directions can be included in the will. Whether they are legally binding depends on the state and the subject of the directions. A recent trend has been for people to give specific directions about the care and transfer of their pets and to fund those directions. In most states these directions are legally binding.

<u>The will doesn't cover everything.</u> Many assets aren't transferred under the terms of your will, and those assets also avoid probate. These include retirement plans, life insurance, annuities, and assets owned by trusts. They are transferred under the terms of the contract involved, which often has a beneficiary designation clause. Every time your will is reviewed, also review how these assets will be distributed.

Strings and conditions. You can put any condition on a gift or bequest as long as it isn't against public policy. Courts generally have allowed any restriction that isn't race-based and doesn't violate or encourage the violation of a law. Some conditions that have been found enforceable in different states include bequests contingent on the beneficiary's being married, staying married, or being employed. There's some question over who will enforce restrictions that apply over time instead of at a point in time. But usually such will provisions are valid.

The Living Trust

A living trust can be a key element of an estate plan. But to be effective it must be properly set up and administered. Many people have living trusts created but don't follow through and use them properly.

A living trust has three significant potential benefits.

The first benefit is that assets owned by the trust avoid probate. Probate is a process under state law that ensures the deceased's debts are paid and that legal title to his or her assets passes to the appropriate people. Avoiding probate often reduces the cost of settling your estate and speeds the transfer of assets to those you want to have them. For many estates, avoiding probate or minimizing the assets that go through probate is an important goal.

The second benefit is that the living trust helps protect your assets during your lifetime and ensure they are managed if there is a time when you aren't able to manage them.

Of course, you should have a power of attorney naming one person or more to handle your affairs when you cannot. The power of attorney is discussed later in this chapter. But a properly set up living trust might result in a better process. A co-trustee or successor trustee takes over management of the trust and its assets when needed.

The third benefit is privacy. A will is a public document that's filed in the courthouse and available for anyone to review. A living trust is a private document that doesn't appear in the public record unless there is litigation involving it. A living trust is a good way to avoid having the details of your estate, and of how you decided to distribute it, made public.

Living trusts can have other potential benefits, but those three are the main ones.

Its full name is the revocable living trust.

Under state law, assets owned by a living trust avoid probate. Legal title passes to the beneficiaries as directed under the trust agreement. That's why a living trust is often called a substitute for a will.

Even if you have a living trust, you should still have a will. You're likely to own some assets that aren't held by the living trust and thus will have to go through probate. In addition, other issues could arise that require someone to be authorized to act on behalf of your estate.

A common mistake is to have a living trust drafted but fail to fully implement it.

Assets avoid probate only when the living trust has legal title to them. With many assets, you must go through the formal process of having the title changed from you as an individual (or from you and your spouse jointly) to the trust. That means contacting financial institutions and having them retitle or transfer ownership of accounts (other than retirement accounts) to the trust. Car and other vehicle registrations should be changed. You might need to change the deeds to your home and any other real estate. Personal property is usually transferred with a simple appendix to the trust that says ownership of all personal property is transferred to the trust.

The more work you do when the trust is created and immediately afterward, the more benefits you and your heirs will receive from the trust.

The Power of Attorney

Many of us won't ever use the power of attorney, and all of us hope it won't ever be needed. Accidents and illnesses happen, unfortunately, and the power of attorney acts as an insurance policy when they do. As with other forms of insurance, the document must be prepared in advance, or it won't be available when it is needed.

What happens to your money and other property if you are disabled and can't manage things? If you have not taken any action, often nothing can happen. Any property that is solely in your name, including your business, legally cannot be sold or managed by anyone other than you. Your family can't use your bank or investment accounts. Bills can't be paid. Investments can't be bought or sold, even if people close to you know that you would have wanted those actions taken. The employees of your business are limited in the actions they can take. Your family can't even borrow against the equity in your home to raise cash for any medical care you might need.

If you become incapacitated and unable to manage your finances, someone needs to step in to pay bills and manage assets. Without a power of attorney, your family would have to go to court and get an order that you are incompetent in order to manage your assets. This procedure can be costly, time-consuming, and potentially embarrassing. In addition, when a court appoints someone to manage your affairs, it is often your closest relative, and that may not be the person you would want to handle your financial affairs.

A power of attorney gives a named person, or persons, known as an attorney-in-fact or agent, the legal right to act for the person who signed the document, known as the principal. A general power of attorney grants the agent the authority to act for the principal in all matters, except any specifically excluded in the document or by state law. A limited power of attorney, as the name implies, grants the power to act on certain specified matters, such as financial affairs, which are named in the document.

A power of attorney can be revoked at any time. The standard power of attorney expires automatically when the person signing the document is incapacitated. Unfortunately, that is the time you most need someone to act for you. That's why the durable power of attorney was developed. If the durable power of attorney is properly drafted, it continues in effect after the person signing it becomes incapacitated. All states now recognize the durable power of attorney. With it, the attorney-in-fact will be able to act when the principal is unable to.

A potential drawback to the durable power of attorney is that it is valid as soon as you sign it, even if you are not incapacitated. There is a possibility that the person named as attorney-in-fact is not trustworthy and could take actions with your assets right away. (On the other hand, it might be better to find that out before you are incapacitated.)

Implementing a power of attorney can be tedious. Most financial services companies have their own forms and will accept only those forms when someone asserts the authority of a power of attorney. You need to contact each financial service company at which you have an account, own a safe deposit box, or have a relationship. Ask what they need to accept someone as an agent under a power of attorney. Unfortunately, your attorney can draft the best power of attorney form and have it be almost useless because your financial institutions insist on their own forms. When you change financial institutions, be sure the new one will accept the agent under your existing power of attorney, or you will need to execute a new one.

The power of attorney can be revoked or modified any time, as long as you are legally competent. It should be reviewed every few years as part of a regular estate plan review. Consider the individual appointed the agent, the powers granted, and whether all appropriate financial institutions have current forms. You also might want to talk with the agent periodically to ensure that your goals and desires for the assets are clear and that he or she is still able and willing to serve.

The Advance Medical Directive

The advance medical directive (AMD) is a specialized power of attorney. It has many variations and names, such as medical care power of attorney and living will. The AMD appoints someone to make health care decisions when you are aren't able to.

For decades, the living will was the primary document. A living will specifies the types of life-saving or life-extending care that you want and don't want. Often it states general principles to guide doctors, and it may state your preferences in some particular situations. A common choice of language is that medical personnel should not use measures that would maintain the principal in "a persistent vegetative state." Living wills are easy to execute. Most states now have standard forms that can be located on the internet.

The problems with living wills are that they are vague, do not cover all circumstances, and cannot keep up with changing medical technology and treatments. Also, surveys show that most living wills don't make their way into the medical charts and have little or no effect on treatment. Doctors either don't know about them, ignore them, or aren't sure how they apply to the current situation.[1]

A health care power of attorney or AMD is a better choice. (These documents are recognized in all states.) Instead of trying to draft general principles to cover all situations, appoint someone who knows you, or multiple people who know you. Your representative or representatives will listen to the medical options and make decisions when you are incapacitated.

The AMD can be personalized and reduces the potential for courts to become involved in your treatment decisions. The power of attorney can be supplemented with a living will or other document that expresses your philosophy and your wishes under various circumstances.

Do Not Resuscitate and Do Not Hospitalize Orders

Do not resuscitate (DNR) and do not hospitalize (DNH) orders are quite common for older people, especially for those who are frail. The reasoning behind signing a DNR is that CPR and similar efforts rarely help elderly and frail individuals recover and instead make their passings violent rather than peaceful. If you don't want to be subject to CPR or similar efforts, execute a DNR and be sure your medical providers have copies.

The reasoning for the DNH is that at some point people do not benefit from hospitalization for every new ailment. Instead, they should be kept comfortable wherever they are residing. Someone who agrees with those sentiments can decline hospitalization in advance by signing a DNH. The reason to sign the document is that you might be unconscious or unable to communicate when people around you have to make a decision. They'll decide to take you to the hospital unless you have a DNH.

Most states have standard forms of DNRs and DNHs that are available on the internet.

HIPAA Authorization

This simple document authorizes medical providers to release medical information about you to the persons you name, without violating the privacy provisions of the Health Insurance Portability and Accountability Act of 1996. HIPAA authorization can be incorporated into an AMD. Many medical providers won't even give details to family members now without express authorization. If you spend time in more than one state, check with an attorney to be sure that your documents will be effective in all states involved.

Other Documents

Documents regarding your care can include non-medical instructions. You can give instructions regarding music, grooming, fresh flowers, and other preferences for your environment when you are receiving care.

Of course, each of your doctors should have a copy of any documents you execute and should also know how to get in touch with the agents named. Each of the agents should also have a copy. Family members should have copies, too, or at least know who the authorized decisionmakers are, even when they aren't the named agents.

Some people appoint the same agent or agents under both the durable power of attorney and their advance medical directive or similar document. Others determine they want different people making the different decisions. The person they want managing their assets isn't the same one they want making care decisions. Determine whether you want the same agent (or the same agents) in both situations or if you want different agents.

The Best Gift to Leave Your Heirs

An essential element of an estate plan that too many people overlook is the instruction letter and inventory. This is a letter, often supplemented by copies of key documents, that tells your executor and anyone else involved in administering your estate everything they need to know to manage your assets and estate.

Without the instruction letter, your executor and survivors could spend weeks or months pulling together the records needed to pay bills and administer and settle your estate. You can avoid problems by leaving even a simple instruction letter that gives your spouse, oldest child, or other key individuals specific information about whom to contact upon your death, the location of your will and other important documents, and perhaps a description of your funeral preferences. Other forms of the letter provide more details, sometimes significantly more. The letter might provide background on special assets you own or your plans for some of the assets. If you have debts, those also should be discussed in detail.

The composition of the estate usually dictates the length and details of the letter. Ideally the letter is accompanied by originals or copies of documents such as financial account statements, deeds, and so forth. The letter and documents should all be included in a notebook. In fact, the letter might not be in the form of a letter. It could be a compilation of documents and details. Included in the package should be a list of your legal and financial advisors, including your attorney, executor, life insurance agent, bank, and other financial institutions. Any other individuals who deal with aspects of your financial situation should be included in the list.

An inventory of your assets, which should also be attached, really is the key to efficient administration of your estate. An inventory has to be done as part of the probate process and also must be done to complete a federal estate tax return and any state version. The process is much easier for the executor and less expensive for the estate if you do the inventory and regularly revise it. You should list what you own and where it or your account statements are located.

Other helpful documents include recent income tax returns, personal financial statements, a list of debts, and an obituary and instructions about where you would like it published. For more valuable estates, the executor would be aided by draft calculations of estate taxes and cash flow.

The inventory should include information about your financial accounts and assets: Social Security, life insurance, pensions, bank accounts, brokerage accounts, mutual funds, and any other assets you own. You could either include the information in the notebook or explain there where files containing the information are located.

If you own special assets, detailed information about those should be provided. This is especially important if you own a small business, a collection, or investment real estate. Often heirs and executors know very little about these items, or at least substantially less than you.

Of course, the instructions and inventory don't have to be in the form of a physical letter and other documents. The information can be provided electronically. You can prepare a spreadsheet of all the assets and debts. Information on how to access online financial accounts can be provided, and any letter or other writing can be in a word-processing file. What's important is that the people who will be managing your assets are given an inventory of the assets and information on how to access and manage them.

A New Estate Planning Rule: Avoid Leaving an Electronic Mess

Many people don't realize the extent of their electronic and digital footprint and the potential problems they're leaving for others to deal with. Estate planning law has mostly caught up to developments in technology, though it took longer than it should have.

Most states have enacted a form of the Uniform Fiduciary Access to Digital Assets Act. Generally, the law allows an executor to manage computer files, web domains, and virtual currencies unless the will or other document specifically prohibits access to them. All the executor has to do is provide proof that he or she is authorized to act as executor. But the law does not give the executor automatic access to email, text messages, social media accounts, and other digital assets. The executor needs express permission in a will, trust, power of attorney, or other legal document or a court order.

Your first step is to be clear in your will, trust, and power of attorney about who should have access to and management ability over each of your digital assets and accounts. Some people divide access to the accounts: They want only a surviving spouse, other family member, or friend to have full access to personal accounts such as email, social media, cell phone, and other similar assets. That person can forward any relevant messages and information to the executor. The executor is given full electronic access to financial accounts and other assets and accounts needed to settle the estate. Other people name an executor to whom they are comfortable giving access and control over all the electronic assets. Decide on the division that works best for you.

But that's only the first and easiest step in digital estate planning. You also need to create a comprehensive inventory of your digital life—and many people are surprised by the extent of this inventory.

A digital asset is any online account or service that is protected by log-in security. Obvious digital assets are email, social media, message board accounts, and subscriptions. Your computer, computer files, files you store on "cloud" accounts and any web domains you own are also digital assets. Financial accounts with online access are of course digital assets. A smart phone and all the apps and other items on it are digital assets. Medical records are being digitized and accessible online, making them part of your digital estate.

Automatic payments are an often forgotten item. Make a list of all your automatic payments, whether they are deducted from a financial account, charged to a payment card, or paid through some other means. Remember that some payments are annual, so your list might not be complete after you have reviewed only one or two months of automatic payments.

Both Apple and Google have legacy contact features that allow you to designate who is allowed access to your phone and other accounts with Apple or Google after you pass away. Facebook (now Meta Platforms) also has such a feature. Be sure to use these in addition to regular estate planning tools.

For other digital assets, list the name and web address of each account or asset and any account number. Include the full name that's on the account, whether it is your name, your spouse's name, both names, or a business name. The inventory also should include all the information needed to gain online access, such as a username or personal ID and the password. If two-factor authentication is used, explain where the authentication is sent. Many digital accounts also have you answer security questions. Include these and your answers in the inventory. Add any other information or comments that may be helpful.

Eight Questions Your Executor and Adult Children Should Be Able to Answer

As part of your estate plan, be sure your adult children and executor are able to answer key questions about you. This information shouldn't be restricted to your estate planning documents. They should have this information while you are healthy so that it will be available should it ever be needed—and it's likely to be needed at different times during your retirement years. At different times family members are likely to have to take you to the doctor or hospital or help you with other matters. They should be able to answer these questions.

<u>What is your personal information?</u> This is a long list. It includes your full name and any previous names, your birthdate, Social Security number, Medicare card information, passport, and any veterans' information. It's also helpful to have a list of previous addresses and your parents' full names. You might not think those are important, but they're very helpful when someone else is trying to obtain authorization to manage your assets or gain online access to one of your accounts. It's also important in regaining access to assets that have been turned over to a state under unclaimed property, or escheat, laws. Any other personal identification information you have is important.

<u>Where are your key documents?</u> These documents include all your estate planning documents, medical records, and all types of insurance policies. Also include documents that support the answers to the first question, such as birth certificates, passports, marriage records, and more.

<u>What should be done if you need help?</u> Where do you want to live? Have you narrowed down a choice of assisted living residences? Or would you prefer to live at home with assistance such as technology, home health care workers, and personal aides? Do you prefer a particular geographic location? If you don't supply these answers, someone else will make all the decisions, and your children are likely to argue over what your preferences are.

<u>How will long-term care be paid for?</u> If you have long-term care insurance, be sure others know about it so that claims are made. Let them know if your plan is to qualify for Medicaid, veterans' aid and assistance, or some other program.

<u>What other insurance do you have?</u> Compile a comprehensive list of all your insurance, including auto, homeowner's, Medicare, additional medical insurance, and life insurance. Don't forget any benefits

you're due from a former employer, from being a veteran, or from any other source.

<u>What estate-planning documents do you have?</u> These include all the documents discussed in this chapter plus any others you have. Be sure to compile an inventory of assets, financial accounts, safe deposit boxes, storage units, and any other assets or information that would be helpful.

<u>What about personal items?</u> You might have a collection, personal mementoes, or other special items that are important to you or that you think might be valuable or important to others. List details: what they are, how valuable they might be, any special instructions on how they should be handled, contacts for knowledgeable people who can help manage the items, and any other helpful information.

<u>What final arrangements do you prefer?</u> Some people have specific preferences about the details of funerals and memorial services, as well as about what is done with their bodies. Whether you do or don't, put it in writing. You don't want loved ones to argue about what you would have wanted. You also might want to write a draft obituary and prepare a list of people or organizations to contact.

Keep in mind that in many states these types of wishes and preferences aren't legally binding. But writing them down gives survivors a guide and minimizes disputes.

CHAPTER 12

The Overlooked Retirement Asset:
Making the Most of Your Home Equity

H ome equity is often one of the worst-managed assets in retire-ment plans. It might be more accurate to say it is one of the least-managed assets.

Most people consider their home equity primarily as something to be left to their children, or tapped in extreme circumstances. Not many people realize that home equity can be used to increase retire-ment cash flow. Even fewer know how to do so efficiently. Often those who plan to make use of some or all of their home equity do so in suboptimal ways, or else fall into traps.

Beating the Downsizing Surprises

Surveys indicate that 40 percent or more of Baby Boomers plan to move sometime after retiring.[1] Most assume they'll lower their living expenses and also extract some equity from the sale of their old homes to help fund retirement.

These all are good plans, but the execution often doesn't generate all the expected benefits. There are oversights, mistakes, and traps that frequently upend the plans and reduce the extent to which moving during retirement increases retirement financial security.

The biggest mistake is to underestimate the costs of downsizing or moving to a lower cost area.

When the plan is to downsize into a smaller home, the amount of personal possessions must be reduced. At a minimum, much personal labor and time are involved in streamlining your possessions. Some people have to pay to have items removed or thrown out. In some cases, professionals are hired to help with the winnowing process. The process of sorting through decades of accumulated items can also be emotional. People who have decumulated, or streamlined, their possessions have told me that you should begin this process at least a couple of years before you plan to move.

After the streamlining is done, the home has to be prepared for sale. Even people who believe they have maintained their homes find after talking to real estate professionals that there's still more work to do. The level and cost of the work required depends on the home's current condition, the state of your local real estate market, and the philosophy of your real estate agent.

There are other costs involved. There will be commissions for the real estate professionals involved. Taxes are likely to be levied by state and local governments. The seller might be responsible for a pest inspection, radon test, and other costs. If you're unsure, ask a real estate professional for a list of the expenses you'll be responsible for.

Another cost is that you have to move the household goods you're keeping to the new home. Many people underestimate this cost, particularly if their employers paid for all or most of the cost of previous moves.

Setting up the new home is another important cost to consider. Many people conclude that after moving they should buy new or additional furniture. Sometimes furniture that fit well in the old, larger home doesn't work in the new, smaller home, or the old stuff now seems too old or out of style for the new place. The point is that you shouldn't assume the furnishings from the old home will move seamlessly to the new home, especially if you're downsizing or moving to a different area of the country. Take a hard-nosed review of how much you'll be able to take to the new home and how much you'll have to pay to outfit the new home.

Three Shrewd Ways Reverse Mortgages Can Enhance Retirement Security

A different way to benefit from your home equity is by using a reverse mortgage, also known as a home equity conversion mortgage (HECM). Forget the negative media on reverse mortgages, and forget the cheesy television commercials promoting reverse mortgages. A reverse mortgage can be a way to use home equity safely and strategically.

Reduce Portfolio Risk

In other chapters I discussed the importance of sequence-of-returns risk and explained how it can derail a retirement plan. The big risk is if a long period of below-average stock returns coincides with the early years of retirement.

In addition to having less money than planned, you would be withdrawing money from the portfolio to pay retirement expenses while the value is down. Unlike during the working years, the entire portfolio won't remain invested so that it can recover with the markets. Because you'd be withdrawing money from the nest egg, it will take a longer and stronger market recovery to return your balance to the level projected in the retirement plan. If the bear market lasts a long time, the retirement plan might never return to expected levels.

This is a situation in which a reverse mortgage can be valuable.

There are several types of reverse mortgages. For this strategy, you want a home equity line of credit (HELOC). For most people it's ideal to set up the reverse mortgage HELOC early in retirement, though it certainly can be set up later. You can initiate the reverse mortgage any time beginning at age sixty-two. There will be set-up costs, but no interest will accrue on the loan until you begin borrowing from the HELOC.

You don't draw from the HELOC while your portfolio is doing well. But should your investments lose value you may not want to draw down the portfolio for the reasons explained above. You want as much money as possible to stay in the portfolio to take advantage of a future market recovery. You instead draw money from the HELOC to help pay retirement expenses. First use any interest and dividend distributions from the portfolio, as well as Social Security and any other regular sources of income, to pay expenses. But then, rather than selling assets to make up any shortfall, draw on the line of credit on your equity in your home.

You can draw on the line of credit until your investment portfolio appreciates to a value at which you're comfortable resuming withdrawals. Then you can stop drawing from the HELOC. You can even repay the HELOC borrowing after the portfolio recovers. Repaying the loans makes it possible to have the maximum line of credit available when the next market downturn occurs. But you don't have to repay any of the loan if you don't want to. Or if you don't think that's the best financial decision. A key advantage of a reverse mortgage HELOC is that you don't have to make any interest or principal payments during your lifetime.

Several studies in recent years have demonstrated that using a reverse mortgage in this way increases long-term growth in the portfolio and reduces the risk of outliving your assets.[2]

The strategy is known as using a reverse mortgage as a "buffer asset," and it is especially valuable to someone whose primary source of retirement income is from 401(k)s or IRAs and whose net worth is $1.5 million or less. Those retirees are most vulnerable to significant bear markets, especially if one occurs early in retirement. But the strategy is valuable for other retirees as well.

Increase Guaranteed Lifetime Income

One way to avoid outliving your money is to have guaranteed lifetime income. Almost all of us have one source of guaranteed lifetime income: Social Security. See chapters 3, 4, and 5 for details about guaranteed lifetime income.

One alternative is to use a reverse mortgage to generate what's called a tenure payment. It's really an income annuity, but the name is different because real estate is involved. Instead of borrowing a lump sum or establishing a HELOC, you set up the reverse mortgage to send you fixed payments for life. You turn your home equity into a guaranteed stream of income.

While that's an attractive strategy, there might be a better one: Set up the reverse mortgage as either a line of credit or a lump sum. Then, take the money from the reverse mortgage and use it to buy a commercial immediate annuity, also known as a single premium immediate annuity (SPIA). See chapter 5 for details about SPIAs.

Most of the time a SPIA will pay you a higher fixed payment for life than the tenure payment from a reverse mortgage. You can determine easily whether that will be the case for you: Shop among reverse mortgage lenders and determine the tenure payment you would receive from them. Also determine the amount you could borrow in a lump sum or using a HELOC, and after learning the lump sum that would be available to you, shop around for annuities and determine the guaranteed lifetime income they would pay you. Shopping for annuities is easy using websites such as www.annuities.direct. Then compare the numbers to determine how to obtain the highest guaranteed lifetime income.

There's a caveat to this strategy, however.

The Department of Housing and Urban Development (HUD), which oversees reverse mortgages, doesn't allow a reverse mortgage to be taken for the purpose of buying an annuity. That's because of some abuses by insurance salespeople in the past. Instead of targeting its rules at the abuses, HUD issued a blanket prohibition against using a reverse mortgage to purchase an annuity.

What this means is that to use this strategy, you need to have additional funds other than the home equity that would be enough to purchase the annuity. For example, you can take money out of your savings or investment portfolio to purchase an annuity and then take money from a reverse mortgage and put it in the investment portfolio to replace the money used to purchase the annuity. Unfortunately, taking out a home equity loan and buying an annuity could be valuable to people who don't have much money outside of their home equity and would like to convert their home equity into guaranteed lifetime income. Because of the HUD rules, they're restricted to taking a tenure payment from a reverse mortgage, though they would receive higher lifetime income by using reverse mortgage proceeds to buy an SPIA.

Delay Claiming Social Security

You maximize lifetime guaranteed and inflation-protected income by delaying Social Security retirement benefits until age seventy. Many people say they can't afford to do that, because they have stopped working and worry about depleting their retirement portfolios if their income isn't supplemented by Social Security.

As discussed in chapter 5, studies demonstrate that it pays off in the long run to take more out of your nest egg to pay expenses early in retirement so you can delay Social Security benefits.

Another option is the reverse mortgage. You can set up a HELOC at age sixty-two or when you retire and take regular withdrawals from the HELOC to help pay living expenses and reduce portfolio withdrawals while delaying Social Security benefits, preferably to age seventy. After claiming Social Security benefits, you can stop taking withdrawals from the HELOC. You might even be able to make repayments on the HELOC so that the loan balance is reduced, and you could then draw from home equity in the future should the need arise.

Reverse Mortgage Basics

When I refer to reverse mortgages in this chapter, I'm talking about federally guaranteed reverse mortgages. A few lenders offer private reverse mortgages, but there aren't many and they don't have some of the advantages of the federally-guaranteed versions. Most importantly, the federally guaranteed reverse mortgages are backed by a reserve fund. When the outstanding balance of a reverse mortgage and accumulated interest and fees exceeds the value of the home, the lender is paid the deficit from the reserve fund. The lender doesn't pursue the homeowner, his or her estate, or the children.

The proceeds of a reverse mortgage are not taxable income either. You're receiving a loan of the equity in your home. You're expected to repay the loan. As far as the tax code is concerned, it is a nontaxable transaction, just as borrowing using a traditional home equity loan is.

After you borrow on a reverse mortgage, interest will accrue on the outstanding loan balance. No payments of interest or principal are due as long as the home is your principal residence. When you pass away or move out of the home, the balance of principal, accumulated interest, and any fees is due. In most cases, the home is sold and the lender is paid from the sale proceeds. If the sale proceeds after costs aren't enough to repay the full amount owed, the government insurance fund pays the difference to the lender. If there's a surplus after the lender is paid, it is distributed according to the terms of your will, living trust, or state law.

A reverse mortgage borrower must be sixty-two years of age or older, and you can only borrow against home equity, so the home should have either no existing mortgage or a small mortgage.

Before taking out a reverse mortgage, you are required to meet with a HUD-approved counselor who must certify that you understand the loan and that you have enough resources to continue paying real estate taxes, homeowner's insurance, and maintenance on the property. The counseling session usually lasts about one hour.

After taking out a reverse mortgage, you are still the homeowner. You live in the home without restrictions as before. You're also responsible for paying all of the expenses of the home. There will be safeguards to ensure you stay current on the real estate taxes and homeowner's insurance. You're free to sell the home, but sale proceeds first go to pay the reverse mortgage balance.

The determination of the maximum amount you can borrow and the interest rate charged can be complicated. Generally, the lower current interest rates are, the more you can borrow. Also, the older you are, the higher the percentage of the home equity you can borrow. There's a dollar limit to the amount you can borrow, regardless of the amount of equity in your home. The limit is adjusted annually for inflation. In 2022 the limit was $970,800.

Because of the way the maximum loan amount is calculated, if you take out a HELOC, the amount you can borrow can increase over time, especially if interest rates increase. I won't go into details here. You can find them in Wade Pfau's book *How to Use Reverse*

Mortgages to Secure Your Retirement or on the website of the U.S. Department of Housing and Urban Development.

You can repay all or part of the amount outstanding on a reverse mortgage at any time.

There are upfront costs to establishing a reverse mortgage. Some are imposed by HUD, and others by the lender. You can pay the upfront costs from your resources or have them added to the reverse mortgage balance. Interest will accumulate if you use the reverse mortgage to pay the fees.

The lender will charge an origination fee, which cannot exceed $6,000. Traditional real estate loan closing costs will also be charged, such as an appraisal fee, title search, recording fee, and others.

HUD charges an initial mortgage insurance premium of 2 percent of the home's appraised value, up to the maximum loan amount. There will also be an annual mortgage insurance premium equal to 0.5 percent of the outstanding balance on the reverse mortgage. The lender is likely to charge annual servicing fees as long as the loan is outstanding.

Shop around before taking out a reverse mortgage. Interest rates and fees vary considerably.

CHAPTER 13

The Solo Years:
When Many Retirement Plans Fail

For married people the most difficult period in retirement is often the solo years, the period after one spouse has passed away. The difficulties of this period can be reduced with proper financial planning, something missing from most retirement plans.

Of course, the solo years are difficult before financial issues are considered. The emotional and personal adjustments for the surviving spouse are significant. Estate planning attorneys over the years have told me that on average it takes a surviving spouse about two years to adjust to the loss of the other spouse. It doesn't matter which spouse passes first, the surviving spouse has to make significant adjustments. I can't offer advice on how to deal with the emotional trials experienced by the surviving spouse, but I can help with the financial issues.

Few retirement plans properly and fully account for the financial changes that occur after one spouse passes away. This oversight increases the stress and pressure on the surviving spouse. My estimate is that when retirement plans fail or falter, they most frequently fail or falter during the solo years. A once-solid plan too often doesn't work as well after one spouse passes away.

Consider these major changes in household finances and management to which most surviving spouses must adapt:

- One Social Security benefit will end.
- Other sources of income, such as pensions and annuities, might end or be reduced.
- Some household expenses are likely to increase. People often have to be hired to do chores and activities that one spouse used to do or which both spouses did together.
- Income taxes are likely to increase, even as income declines.

Those are the broadly universal changes that occur after one spouse passes away, but some surviving spouses face other changes and adjustments unique to their situations.

The consequences of these challenges depend on two factors.

One factor is the extent of the surviving spouse's knowledge of and comfort with the household finances. Many married couples have a division of labor, and part of the division is that one spouse handles the finances and makes most of the financial decisions. That works well as long as they are a couple, but it becomes a serious problem when the spouse who handles the finances is the first to pass away. As retirement progresses, the spouse who isn't primarily involved in the finances needs to be fully informed about the basics of managing finances and what actions need to be taken if the financial-manager spouse passes away. The non-financial spouse needs to become knowledgeable of finances and comfortable with the management.

An alternative is for the financial-manager spouse to bring another person up to speed on the management of the household finances to plan for the solo years. A good candidate is the agent (or agents) under the power of attorney or successor trustee (or trustees) of the revocable living trust. It makes a lot of sense for this person (or these people) to be familiar with the finances before their services are really needed. A good strategy is for the financial-manager spouse to begin transitioning management of the finances to the chosen successor. An alternative is to let the person know where the information needed to manage the household finances is located.

The other factor is how much thought was given to the solo years when the retirement plan was developed and revised. The changes that will occur after one spouse's demise should be identified, such as the loss of one Social Security benefit and any other declines in income. Increases in household expenses also should be anticipated and estimated. These changes can be less certain, but attempts should be made to identify areas in which a surviving spouse is likely to need help in maintaining and managing the household. The couple also should consider whether a surviving spouse should sell the current home.

The two most important financial consequences of the solo years are changes in federal income taxes and the Social Security benefits available to the surviving spouse.

The Widow's Penalty Tax

Many surviving spouses are surprised to find that federal income taxes can increase substantially after one spouse passes away, even if there has been a decline in household income. This doesn't happen to all surviving spouses, but it happens to enough that tax and financial planners call the phenomenon the widow's penalty tax.

Despite the name, income taxes are likely to increase whether the surviving spouse is a man or a woman because of what is more accurately called the surviving spouse's penalty tax. The less the income declines, the more significant the tax penalty is. This isn't a separate penalty in the tax code, such as the penalty for underpaying estimated taxes, rather, it's a consequence of the way the tax code is written and how it interacts with the changes that occur after one spouse passes away.

Here's how the surviving spouse's penalty works.

When both spouses are alive, the couple's tax return filing status is married filing jointly. A surviving spouse is allowed to use the married filing jointly filing status only for the year in which the other spouse died. Beginning the first full year after one spouse passes away, the surviving spouse's filing status changes to single. Married filing jointly is the most beneficial status while the single filing status is comparatively unfavorable.

There is a surviving spouse filing status, but only a limited number of taxpayers qualify for it, and they are generally younger people than retirees.

Here's how the change in filing status affects a surviving spouse.

In 2022, taxpayers who were married filing jointly stayed in the 12 percent tax bracket until their taxable income exceeded $83,550. But a single taxpayer stayed in the 12 percent bracket only until his or her taxable income exceeded $41,775. The 22 percent tax bracket applied to a married couple filing jointly until taxable income exceeded $178,150, but for a single taxpayer the ceiling for the 22 percent bracket was taxable income of $89,075. (The break points of the income tax brackets change each year because of inflation adjustments. So the details change from year to year. But the basic effects are the same.)

You can see that the surviving spouse is hit with a double whammy.

First, as I said earlier, income is likely to decline. Second, the surviving spouse is pushed into a higher tax bracket. The income usually doesn't decline enough to keep the surviving spouse in the same tax bracket after becoming a single taxpayer. If it did, that would be a very significant decline, to halve the couple's income before the death of the spouse. More typically, the surviving spouse loses some income but also pays a higher income tax rate on the remaining income because of the change in filing status.

Here's an example. Suppose Max and Rosie had a taxable income of $120,000, resulting in a federal income tax of $17,634 in 2022. Max passes away. In her first full year as a widow, Rosie's taxable income is $100,000. As a single taxpayer she's now in the 24 percent tax bracket instead of the 22 percent bracket, as when she and Max were filing joint returns. Rosie's federal income taxes on the lower income are $28,760.50, using 2022 tax tables. (The results will be a little different in real life, because the tax tables are adjusted for inflation each year.)

Income declines, but taxes on the remaining income increase.

That's not the only federal tax penalty on a surviving spouse. As we have seen, Medicare beneficiaries with higher incomes are subject to a Medicare premium surtax, also known as IRMAA (income-related monthly adjustment amount). The higher a beneficiary's modified adjusted gross income, the more Medicare premiums increase. (More details about IRMAA are in chapters 7 and 10.)

As with income taxes, the Medicare premium surtax is imposed at different income levels on people with different tax filing statuses. A single taxpayer with the same modified adjusted gross income as a married couple will pay twice the Medicare surtax as the couple. A newly widowed taxpayer who retains a high percentage of the couple's previous income could pay a Medicare premium surtax, exceeding what the couple paid jointly.

Higher income taxes on Social Security benefits could be another survivor's penalty tax. A portion of Social Security benefits is included in gross income when MAGI is above a certain level, and the amount of benefits included in gross income increases as modified adjusted income increases. Unlike the other taxes, the trigger points for the inclusion of Social Security benefits in gross income aren't adjusted for inflation each year. That means that as inflation increases, more and more people are required to include Social Security benefits in gross income, and within a few years about 80 percent of Social Security beneficiaries will pay income taxes on a portion of their benefits. (Details about income taxes on Social Security benefits can be found in chapter 10.)

Survivor's Social Security Benefits

Surviving spouses are in a unique position under Social Security and need to know the special rules and options regarding survivor's benefits, also known as widow's benefits. It's especially important for surviving spouses between ages sixty and seventy to consider their options carefully. Unlike other Social Security beneficiaries, a surviving spouse is able to choose one type of benefits and later change to another type of benefits. The decisions made after one spouse passes away can make a substantial difference in the lifetime income of the surviving spouse. The choices facing the surviving spouse can also be among the more difficult Social Security decisions.

It's important to emphasize that married couples should coordinate their benefit decisions and consider the solo years when choosing when to claim their retirement benefits. Coordinated decisions between spouses make it possible for the survivor, whichever spouse it is, to receive the maximum possible from Social Security for the rest of his or her life. When spouses don't coordinate benefits, the surviving spouse often finds that the one benefit check supporting the household is substantially less than it could have been if different decisions had been made years earlier. (I discussed the different claiming options and strategies for Social Security retirement benefits in chapter 4.)

Survivor's Benefit Basics

Survivor's benefits are available to both married and divorced widows and widowers. That means a divorced person might qualify to receive survivor's benefits after the ex-spouse passes away, though they no longer are married. To minimize confusion, however, this chapter will focus on survivor's benefits available to someone who was married at the time the other spouse passed away.

Social Security's data say that about 80 percent of surviving spouse benefits are paid to women, which is why the benefit is known as the widow's benefit. The surviving spouse is likely to be the wife. So in my discussion and examples in this chapter, I'll assume the deceased spouse was a husband and the surviving spouse is a wife. But the same rules apply in other situations.

To qualify for survivor's benefits, you must be a widow or widower who was married to the deceased spouse for at least the nine months immediately before the deceased spouse passed away. The nine-month requirement is waived if the deceased spouse's death was accidental. In addition, for the survivor to claim benefits the deceased spouse must have been fully insured under Social Security. This generally means the deceased spouse must have earned a minimum amount of income in jobs covered by Social Security for at least ten years.

A qualified surviving spouse of a fully insured worker can claim survivor's benefits as early as age sixty, or age fifty if the survivor is disabled and the disability started before or within seven years of the other spouse's death. Keep in mind that, although you are allowed to begin receiving survivor's benefits as early as age sixty, you'll receive lower benefits than would be paid if you waited to receive them at a later age. The benefits are reduced by 0.396 percent for each month you claim them before your full retirement age. The reduction comes to 4.75 percent for each year. If your FRA is sixty-six, the maximum reduction, incurred by claiming the benefits at age sixty, is 28.5 percent.

Survivor's Benefits Have Many Levels

The amount of survivor's benefits you're eligible for depends on your age, the deceased spouse's earnings record, and the age and benefit status of the deceased spouse at the time of his passing. These variables can create a range of benefit choices for the surviving spouse. I'll break down the different benefit levels and options.

The Deceased Spouse Was Younger than Sixty-Two

If the deceased spouse passed away before age sixty-two, he didn't have the opportunity to claim retirement benefits. But the survivor's benefits will be based on the deceased spouse's earnings record.

The surviving spouse has two immediate claiming options. She can claim the survivor's benefits based on the deceased spouse's full retirement benefit. The survivor's benefits can be claimed as early as age sixty. The other option is for the surviving spouse to claim her own earned retirement benefits, which can be done as early as age sixty-two. Keep in mind that if you claim either of these benefits before your FRA, the benefits, whether survivor's benefits or retirement benefits, will be reduced. The longer they are claimed before your FRA, the lower the benefits will be.

Unlike in many other situations, the surviving spouse can choose to claim one type of benefit initially and later can switch to another, after delaying her claim for the second benefit until she will receive the maximum amount for it. Later in this chapter I discuss how to maximize benefits using this powerful option.

The Deceased Spouse Was at Least Sixty-Two and Had Claimed Benefits

When your spouse passes away after age sixty-two and had claimed retirement benefits before his full retirement age, you can claim survivor's benefits based on his work history. But the benefits will be reduced below his FRA amount, because he claimed his benefits early.

Again, the surviving spouse has the choice of receiving the survivor's benefits as early as age sixty, or at a later age. If the surviving spouse elects to claim benefits before her full retirement age, the amount of the benefits will be reduced for each month before FRA that they are claimed. This reduction is in addition to the reduction that is made because the deceased spouse claimed benefits before his FRA.

The surviving spouse can increase the benefit by delaying its start. The amount is increased gradually for each month the claim is delayed.

This is where things can become complicated for a surviving spouse. Social Security has a special formula that limits the benefits paid to a surviving spouse whose deceased spouse claimed retirement benefits before his FRA. The formula is called the Retirement Insurance Benefit Limit, or RIB-LIM. Some also call it the widow's limit. SSA says about one-third of surviving spouses receive reduced benefits because of RIB-LIM. The result of the formula is that the maximum the surviving spouse will receive is the higher of the amount the deceased spouse was receiving at the time of his demise or 82.5 percent of his FRB. The closer to your full retirement age that you claim the survivor's benefits, the more likely your benefit is to be reduced by RIB-LIM. At some point before your FRA the benefit amount might be maximized, because the benefit can't be more than 82.5 percent of the deceased spouse's FRB or what he was receiving when he died.

You don't need to know the details of how the RIB-LIM is calculated and applied. You need to know that if you're a surviving spouse and the deceased spouse claimed benefits before FRA, then the limit might apply to you.

There are several ways you can determine how your benefits will be reduced and when you'll reach the crossover point after which survivor's benefits won't increase with any further delay in claiming them. You can work with SSA representatives, either on the telephone or at the local office, or you can open a "my Social Security" account on the Social Security web site and use the online calculator to estimate the benefits under different scenarios. You can also purchase one of the commercial software programs discussed near the end of chapter 5. Another option is to work with a financial planner with expertise in Social Security benefits.

When the RIB-LIM applies, the surviving spouse needs to consider a two-step strategy. The strategy is most likely to be beneficial when the surviving spouse has retirement benefits based on her own work history and they aren't substantially lower than her late husband's benefits. In this situation, it can make sense to claim survivor's benefits initially. Then, after the surviving spouse's FRA and preferably at age seventy, the surviving spouse switches over to his or her own retirement benefits. At that point the retirement benefits may have increased to the point that they are higher than the survivor's benefits. The reverse strategy also should be reviewed and considered.

The Deceased Spouse Was Older than Sixty-Two and Had Not Claimed Benefits

There are two scenarios in this situation.

The first scenario is that your spouse passed away before his full retirement age and he had not claimed benefits. In this case, you'll receive his earned FRB.

The second scenario is that your spouse passed away after reaching his FRA and still had not claimed benefits. In that case, you'll receive whatever he would have received, including delayed retirement credits, as if he had applied for retirement benefits on the day he died.

But in either case the final amount paid to you is reduced if you claim the survivor's benefits before your own FRA.

The Deceased Spouse Was Older than Full Retirement Age and Receiving Benefits That Were Claimed at FRA or Later

This is another fairly simple situation. In this case the surviving spouse receives the amount the deceased spouse was receiving at the time of his death. But don't forget that the survivor's benefit is reduced if the surviving spouse claims the survivor's benefits before her FRA.

Why Delaying Retirement Benefits Matters

As I've said, after one spouse passes away, only one Social Security check comes into the household of the surviving spouse. In most cases, the amount paid to the survivor is the higher of the survivor's benefits as outlined above and the surviving spouse's own earned retirement benefits. As you can tell from the examples above, it's important for the higher-earning spouse to delay receiving retirement benefits as long as possible, because the benefit the higher-earning spouse was receiving or would have been entitled to at full retirement age is likely to be the basis of the survivor's benefit.

The surviving spouse's household income is already going to be reduced, because the passing of one spouse eliminates one monthly benefit. If the higher-earning spouse claimed benefits before FRA, then the income to the survivor is reduced below what it could have been if the higher-earning spouse had claimed at FRA or later. Even if the surviving spouse is the higher-earning spouse, he or she is likely to wish that the benefits claim had been delayed so a higher benefit would be coming in to the household.

Which Benefits to Claim and When to Claim Them

A surviving spouse has the most options available between the ages of sixty and seventy. She can choose between her own retirement benefit and the survivor's benefit. Later, she can switch to the other benefit. A switch is likely to make sense, because whichever benefit is received second is likely to be higher than it would have been initially if she waits to claim it until her own full retirement age or later.

A good general rule for a surviving spouse is to determine which benefit will top out at the highest level at her FRA or later, and then delay taking that benefit until it is maximized.

Another point is that it is important to compare the numbers over the long term. Most people, based on Social Security Administration data, take the highest benefit available at the time they claim benefits and then don't revisit the decision. But by doing that they might short-change themselves. The longer the survivor lives, the more money she will leave on the table by not making the optimum decision and by not considering the option to change benefits.

The Cheapest Life Insurance

The important point to note is that if the husband (assuming he's the higher-earning spouse) claims his retirement benefits before his FRA, the widow will never receive more than 82.5 percent of his FRB. Because so many people claim their retirement benefits before reaching FRA, Social Security data say that about 60 percent of widows receive survivor's benefits that are less than what their late husband's benefit would have been at his FRA.

That's why I emphasize that in married couples the higher earning spouse should delay receiving retirement benefits as long as possible. In most marriages, at least one of the spouses is likely to live longer than average life expectancy. There's a significant probability that at least one spouse will live well beyond average life expectancy for the age group. That surviving spouse will receive only one Social Security check. Unless the couple has such substantial assets and income that Social Security benefits aren't significant to them, it makes sense to ensure that you make the most out of your survivor's check.

The higher-earning spouse should think of delaying the retirement benefit as a very affordable life insurance policy. The delay will increase the amount paid to the surviving spouse every month for life, no matter how long that life lasts. The longer the surviving spouse lives, the longer that higher benefit will be received. Most people don't realize the value of that benefit. You would have to purchase a significant life insurance policy to fund an annuity that would pay the higher benefit amount indexed for inflation and guaranteed for life. It's much more affordable to delay retirement benefits for a few years.

Social Security is an insurance program, and it primarily is insurance against living a long life. Unless there's a significant probability that neither spouse will live to at least average life expectancy, maximize the longevity insurance benefit by delaying the benefits of the higher-earner in the couple.

What Happens When a Widow Remarries?

We've looked at the survivor's benefits available to a widowed person based on the deceased spouse's earnings and claiming history. But what about when a widow or widower remarries? How does that affect the choices?

If a widow remarries after age sixty, there is no change. She is still entitled to survivor's benefits based on her previous deceased spouse's earnings and claiming record.

Because of this rule, some surviving spouses are entitled to claim benefits based on the earnings records of more than one spouse. The survivor will receive only one check at a time, but she can compare several spouse's earnings histories to maximize benefits.

For example, suppose you were widowed in your early sixties and began collecting survivor's benefits on your late husband's earnings history. Then you remarry after your full retirement age. At that point you can switch to a spousal benefit based on your new husband's earnings record and will receive it if it is higher than your current survivor's benefit. Your spousal benefit won't be reduced for early claiming, because you have reached your FRA. The fact that you claimed the survivor's benefit from the previous marriage before your FRA won't carry over to reduce the new spousal benefit.

If the second spouse passes away before you, you can claim survivor's benefits based on either of the two deceased spouses, and you will receive the higher of the two benefits.

None of this applies if you remarry before age sixty. In that case, you're not entitled to survivor's benefits from the first husband unless the second marriage ends by divorce, death, or annulment. In those cases you might be eligible for survivor's benefits from the first spouse's earnings record.

The same rules apply to disabled spouses, except they can begin survivor's benefits as early as age fifty.

Widows Beware

You can't depend on the Social Security Administration for the right answers. It's unfortunate, but it has been shown that too often SSA reps give the wrong answers when asked about benefits.

Unfortunately, surviving spouses have been some of the leading recipients of bad advice and service from the SSA. In 2018 a report from the Office of the Inspector General of SSA concluded that SSA systematically failed to inform surviving spouses of their benefit choices. As a result, 82 percent of surviving spouses were underpaid, receiving lower benefits than they were eligible for. Specifically, SSA didn't inform surviving spouses that they could delay their own retirement benefits until age seventy while claiming survivor's benefits in the interim.

The lesson here is that Social Security is complicated and you can't rely on the SSA to give you accurate and complete advice. Educate yourself about the options and seek help from knowledgeable sources to ensure that your lifetime guaranteed benefits are maximized.

I discuss Social Security benefits in general and survivor's benefits in particular in my book, *Where's My Money? Secrets to Getting the Most out of Your Social Security* (Regnery Capital, 2021). The book includes numerous examples alongside more detailed rules and explanations to help you understand Social Security.

Plan for the Solo Years

Many people downplay the widow's tax and other consequences of the solo years. They say the problems will last for only a few years at most, and then the surviving spouse will pass away. Yet we know that in 75 percent of married couples one spouse will outlive the other by at least five years. In about 50 percent of couples, one spouse will outlive the other by at least ten years.[1]

Be sure to consider all the potential ramifications of the solo years, run the numbers, and learn the potential extent of the problem. Estimate how much the income will decline after one spouse passes away. Then estimate how much taxes and other expenses will increase, being sure to estimate the taxes after the transition to single filing status. Don't forget to estimate the Stealth Taxes, such as the Medicare premium surtax and taxes on Social Security benefits. See chapter 11 for more details about these and other Stealth Taxes.

You may decide to spend less in the years before one spouse passes away to ensure that more money is available for the solo years. Some people will buy permanent life insurance to provide a lump sum of tax-free cash to the surviving spouse.

Another strategy is to increase future tax-free income. The widow's penalty tax and the other Stealth Taxes of the solo years are good reasons to consider converting at least part of a traditional IRA to a Roth IRA now. Pay the taxes now at the lower married filing jointly rate to provide tax-free income in the future when the surviving spouse is likely to be in a higher income tax bracket as a single taxpayer.

CHAPTER 14

Do Retirees Have Too Much Invested in Stocks? (and Other Investment Issues)

I nvestment risks multiply for retirees and those near retirement, because they have less time for their portfolio values to recover from market declines and investment mistakes. If a retiree invests too conservatively, the portfolio might be less likely to achieve high enough returns to sustain a retirement that could last twenty, thirty, or more years. Yet if a retiree invests too aggressively, losses could be incurred that increase the probability of running out of money in retirement.

To deal with these opposing risks, two broad investment strategies are typically recommended to retirees.

The traditional strategy is that as a person approaches retirement, he or she should reduce the risk in the investment portfolio. Most of the portfolio should be moved to bonds, certificates of deposit, and other safe, liquid investments that pay interest and don't risk losing significant value in a declining stock market. This traditional strategy became less popular after interest rates began declining in the 1980s, and especially after rates fell to new lows in the late 1990s. As rates declined even more following the financial crisis of 2007–08, interest rates on bonds and other traditional conservative investments for retirees were too low to generate adequate income. Today, most retirees don't have enough investment capital to generate sufficient income using this strategy.

The alternative investment strategy that has probably been recommended most often to retirees in the last twenty years or so is the total-return or diversified portfolio approach. The portfolio isn't changed much as a person approaches or enters retirement. As in the pre-retirement years, the nest egg is invested in a diversified portfolio that's designed to achieve growth over time. The percentage that is invested in stocks or other risky assets might be reduced as retirement nears, but not significantly below the allocation during the working years.

The idea behind the total-return approach is to continue investing for the long term, because for most people retirement is likely to last twenty years or longer. The retiree sets a policy for withdrawing money to spend, as described in chapter 6. The portfolio will decline in value at times, but it will recover when markets recover. If investments earn their historic average returns during retirement, the retiree will have more money to spend in the long term than he or she would from using the traditional approach.

There are several ways recommended for allocating assets in the total return portfolio.

A longstanding approach to asset allocation is a simple formula: the percentage of stocks in the portfolio is 100 minus the individual's age. Some people use 110 instead of 100. If the retiree is sixty-five, then 35 percent of the portfolio is in stocks, and the rest is in bonds or other safe investments. As the individual ages, the percentage held in stocks declines.

Another method is the classic balanced portfolio. This portfolio is allocated 60 percent to stocks and 40 percent to bonds. Some advisers say that as a person nears or enters retirement, the percentages should be flipped to 40 percent stocks and 60 percent bonds.

More recently, investment firms and advisers have developed sophisticated analytical tools to determine the recommended asset allocation for a portfolio. The allocation is based on an individual's goals, risk tolerance, and other factors. It changes over time as a person ages, markets fluctuate, and as other circumstances change. Likewise, there is a type of mutual fund known as a target date fund.

The investment results of these and other strategies depend on the investment environment the retiree encounters. In the next section of this chapter I discuss the sequence-of-returns risk in detail, one of the most important factors to consider when selecting an investment strategy for retirement.

Why Asset Allocation Matters: Sequence-of-Returns Risk

People planning for retirement in their twenties, thirties, and even forties are told to invest primarily in stocks. Stocks earn the highest returns in the long term. Stock prices will decline at times during the working years, but they'll eventually recover, and over the long term, even after accounting for those bear markets, stocks will deliver a higher return and more money than other investments. When stock prices do decline during the working years, the individual will be buying more stocks at lower prices with regular contributions to the 401(k) or other account through which he or she is saving and investing.

But we have seen that there is a potential problem with that approach as retirement approaches and in the early years of retirement. What economists call sequence-of-returns can derail a retirement. It matters most in the ten years that includes the five years before and the five years after retirement, which is sometimes called the retirement danger zone, the retirement-risk zone, or the window of vulnerability.

Stocks and other risky investments don't earn steady returns from year to year. U.S. stock indices have an average annual return over the long term of about 10 percent. But they rarely return 10 percent in a year. Most years, the return is well above or well below 10 percent. Many years of different levels of returns are compiled to arrive at the long-term average.

Stocks have a history of bull markets and bear markets, long periods when their returns are well above, or well below, the long-term average. Bull markets and bear markets can last ten to twenty years. In a bull market the total return approach will earn a much higher return than the long-term average, which would leave the retiree much better off financially than expected. But when a long-term bear market occurs in the early years of retirement, a retiree using the total return approach or the classic 60–40 portfolio will earn below-average returns for years, leaving the retiree much worse off than expected and substantially increasing the risk of running out of money.

Sequence-of-returns risk is especially dangerous for those near retirement age, because that is when the retirement nest egg is likely to be at its highest level. Also, the individual is about to stop earning money from work and along with it the ability to add savings to the fund when the investment values decline.

In addition, the retiree will be withdrawing principal from the portfolio. That money won't be in the portfolio to increase in value when the markets recover. For the portfolio to return to its previous level, the assets remaining in the portfolio would have to earn even higher returns in the future.

A retirement plan projects that the investment portfolio will generate a cash flow, and the projection assumes that the portfolio will earn a particular average rate of return. If the portfolio value declines during the first years of retirement because of bad investment returns, the retirement plan will be off track from the start.

Financial researchers such as Wade Pfau estimate that about 80 percent of the variation in the amount of money available for retirees to distribute from their nest eggs is due to differences in investment returns.[1] The investment returns during the retirement window of vulnerability can determine the success or failure of a retirement plan and may require meaningful changes in spending plans.

Sequence-of-Returns Risk: Real-World Examples

The potential for investment returns to derail a retirement plan aren't theoretical. Bear markets and periods of below-average returns happen frequently. As I discuss in chapter 1, they have a higher probability of occurring in the 2020s and probably into the 2030s. Here are some examples of how sequence-of-returns risk has been realized in the past.

U.S. stock indices generated higher than average returns during the 1990s, especially the last years of the 1990s. Stock indices set new record highs regularly, and investors increased their allocations to stocks. We refer to this period now as the technology stock bubble, because technology stocks had higher returns than other sectors of the market. But those stocks soon gave up a lot of those gains.

The S&P 500 stock index was around 1400 in early 2000. By September 2002 the S&P 500 reached a bear market low of 815. The index began to recover and reached a new record high of 1556 in October 2007. Unfortunately, that was the beginning of what we now know as the financial crisis. Stocks declined sharply again and didn't reach a bottom until March 2009, at 676.

Stocks began to recover in March 2009, but the S&P 500 didn't return to its previous high until March 2013. The returns were even worse for investors in the Nasdaq 100, a more volatile index that has a higher allocation to technology stocks.

You can see that a retiree who invested primarily in stocks didn't have a cumulative positive return from early 2000 through March 2013. In the meantime, the retiree had to spend from the portfolio to pay living expenses.

A similar sequence of returns occurred from 1968 through 1982. During that period, both stocks and bonds declined because the economy experienced high inflation and low economic growth simultaneously. A study by T. Rowe Price Associates found that the actual returns of a typical total return portfolio during that period were much less than the historic average. In fact, as I reported in the first edition of my book *The New Rules of Retirement*, the T. Rowe Price study found that someone who retired in 1968, invested in a total return portfolio, and used the 4 percent rule to withdraw money from the portfolio would run out of money before the end of 1983, just as the long bull market in stocks and bonds was beginning.[2] (For details about the 4 percent rule, see chapter 6.)

Ways to Beat Sequence-of-Returns Risk

Fortunately, there are ways to deal with the sequence-of-returns risk.

One strategy is to replace your working career paycheck with a retirement paycheck by establishing guaranteed lifetime income. I explain the importance of doing this in chapter 3 and how to do it in chapters 4 and 5. Another strategy is to establish a better spending plan for the portion of your nest egg that's invested. In chapter 6, I explain different ways to create a spending plan and the importance of having a spending plan that adjusts for inflation and changes in the markets.

You also should consider adjusting your investment strategy to reduce your vulnerability to sequence-of-returns risk. As I said, today most retirees are advised to follow the total-return approach and have portfolios invested primarily in stocks and bonds. These portfolios are highly correlated to the stock indices for both their returns and their volatility. They do well when stock indices do well, but poorly during bear markets in stocks. They don't really provide the diversification investors expect, as I explain in more detail in chapter 2, where I also discuss alternative investment strategies to consider. Additional strategies for creating a more diversified portfolio have been proposed by Craig Israelsen and Alex Shahidi.[3]

Another strategy that has received some attention is known as the rising-equity glidepath, or the U-shaped equity glidepath. It is the opposite of one of the traditional recommendations for retirees. The investor reduces the stock allocation to 30 percent or less by the retirement date. After retirement, the investor steadily increases the stock allocation by one or two percentage points each year. Under this strategy, the individual has a low allocation to stocks during the critical ten years around the retirement date. The stock allocation steadily increases as the high-risk period passes, enabling the retiree to earn higher returns through most of retirement.[4]

The strategy generates less wealth when stocks are in a bull market during the early years of retirement but does much better than traditional strategies when the early years of retirement coincide with a bear market. It is a defensive strategy.

Find the Best Strategy for You

The only way to know for certain which is the best investment strategy for your retirement is to be able to forecast investment returns for the first five to ten years of your retirement. You aren't likely to be able to do that so you need to focus on probabilities for the next few years and decide what risks you're willing to take, and what risks you want to avoid.

Your first decision should be whether you want a relatively fixed asset allocation or one that you're going to change during retirement.

If you choose a fixed asset allocation, choose one that's likely to do well in most economic environments. For example, the traditional allocation of 60 percent stocks and 40 percent bonds does very well when stocks are delivering average or better returns, but it doesn't do well at other times. While it is considered a diversified portfolio by most people, it's heavily correlated with the stock indices. To achieve real diversification in your portfolio, consider the portfolios recommended by Craig Israelsen and Alex Shahidi. Or consider the True Diversification model portfolio published in my Retirement Watch newsletter.

If you don't want a fixed asset allocation, develop a strategy to change the allocation over time. You could establish a mechanical way to change the allocation. For example, the rising equity glidepath strategy reduces the stock allocation as retirement approaches and gradually increases the stock allocation after that. The stock allocation is increased by a fixed percentage each year without regard to what's happening in the investment markets.

Or you might prefer a less mechanical strategy that adjusts based on developing economic circumstances. As I discuss in chapter 2, you're likely to need the assistance of a financial professional to execute such a strategy successfully.

The investment environment that exists when you approach retirement and are in the early years of retirement will determine how well the strategy you select works. While you can't successfully forecast investment returns, you can develop an idea of how likely it is that investment returns will be higher or lower than the long-term average in the near future. You can look at interest rates, inflation rates, stock market valuations compared to historic levels, and other factors. You also can look at returns over the last five to ten years and estimate whether those are likely to continue or are more likely to reverse course. In chapter 1 I listed reasons to expect investment returns in the next five to ten years to be lower than in the years that immediately preceded.

Most people should enlist the help of an investment advisor, financial planner, or other financial professional when determining their investment strategies. A significant benefit from working with a financial advisor is that you're less likely to make a sharp reversal in your investment strategy when there's a significant but short-term change in the markets or economy.

CHAPTER 15

How to Avoid the Major Causes of Retirement Failure and Achieve True Success in Retirement

Many retirement plans fail. They didn't have to. They failed because of actions or inactions by the retiree, not uncontrollable outside forces. Fortunately, these retirement failures are fairly easy to avoid. Most people just need to do work they didn't consider before retirement. But many in retirement don't even realize what needs to be done.

I focus primarily on retirement finances in this book, in my newsletter Retirement Watch, and in my online seminars, the Spotlight Series. While solid finances are an important part of being independent and secure in retirement, they aren't enough. Solid finances give you confidence, but they don't make you happy or satisfied. In fact, many people who are financially secure fail at retirement while others who are much less financially secure have successful retirements.

A failed retirement is one in which the retiree is not satisfied and secure. Life satisfaction is the goal. That's why you saved and invested during the working years.

Whether you are already retired or are still planning for it, you need to identify the reasons why retirement could fail and take appropriate actions to avoid failure in order to have a satisfying retirement.

The Stress of Retirement

Few people realize it, but retirement can be stressful, even before considering finances.

A couple of psychologists developed the Holmes and Rahe Stress Scale, also known as the Social Readjustment Rating Scale, to measure the level of stress people experienced or felt from different life events. Holmes and Rahe listed forty-three significant common life events and used their scale to rank the relative stress levels of the events.

Retirement was the tenth most stressful of the forty-three events. In addition, events associated with retirement or that are likely to occur during retirement make up about twenty of the other forty-two events. These events include losing work or having a change in work, the death of a spouse, a change in marital status, change in the health of a family member, a change in living conditions, a change in residence, and more.[1]

The notion that retirement can be stressful in general and that there can be multiple stressful events during retirement differs greatly from the popular view of retirement promoted by many in the retirement industry. The gap between the image and the reality is a major reason for retirement failure. Too many people aren't prepared for some of the realities of retirement and don't realize the importance of the non-financial aspects of retirement.

A successful retirement means more than a healthy balance sheet and income statement. In fact, wealthier retirees aren't happier than others, according to surveys taken by financial advisor Wes Moss.[2] After a point, happiness and a successful retirement aren't about the money.

Retirees in general suffer more from certain problems than the rest of the population. Those sixty-five and older are more likely than the general population to commit suicide, engage in substance abuse, be depressed, and experience a range of other social problems. Conduct an internet search on any of those topics, and you'll find data confirming that older people are more likely to have these issues and that their prevalence among those sixty-five and older is increasing.

The Soft Side of Retirement

You can have a satisfying, happy, and successful retirement but you need to approach retirement with more than finances in mind. You must address the personal, nonfinancial problems of retirement, or what I call the soft side of retirement.

The most important part of retirement is how you spend your time. Before retirement, how you spent most of your time was decided for you. Work and career took a large chunk of your time. Work was a large part of your identity and sense of worth and purpose. You were probably also raising children. Very little of your time was free to use as you pleased, so it was easy to decide what to do during that limited time.

All that ends for most people during retirement. The time you spent working, raising children, and in some other activities is now free time. That's a great feeling at first, but it's a lot of time to fill. Failure to fill this time in productive, and fulfilling ways can lead to failed retirements.

Many people enter retirement focused on what they are gaining, such as reduced stress and the time to pursue activities they've put off for a long time. But you're also losing a lot when you leave the workplace. Work provided structure to at least five days of the week and really provided the weekly structure. Work also provided purpose and fulfillment and let you achieve goals. For most people, work provided a lot of social contacts and structure. You lose all these things when you retire, and many people don't realize what they're losing until well after they retire.

There's an initial period, often called the retirement honeymoon, when the person relaxes because they don't have to go to work and deal with its various stresses. They can devote time to personal activities they long wanted or needed to do.

The honeymoon can last from a few months to a few years. But eventually the pent-up activities are done, and the reality of what's lost hits home. A retirement routine begins.

The first years of the pandemic gave many pre-retirees a flavor of retirement and the opportunity to practice retirement part time. They had more free time and were spending more time at home. They had less contact with co-workers, and what contact they had was through electronic means. The pandemic gave people a sample of what they would miss in retirement. They learned what life is like when they aren't in the work place.

The good news is that there are effective road maps for how to be successful with the soft side of retirement. Unlike with a lot of the financial issues, the route to a successful, happy retirement is pretty much the same for most people. There has been a lot of research conducted over the decades, and it shows the keys to satisfaction, happiness, and health during the post-career years.

It's time to follow the road map to retirement success if you haven't already started. It doesn't matter when you begin on this part of retirement planning. Whether it's at the beginning of retirement or after you've been retired for years, following these steps will lead to retirement success.

The Social Imperative

Social interaction and a social life are very important to both mental and physical health as we age. The evidence of the importance of regular social interactions is overwhelming. Relationships are a key to good mental and physical health, and having some close, satisfying relationships is very important.

The Harvard Study of Adult Development has been ongoing for almost eighty-five years. The Harvard Study doesn't survey different people or random people. It surveys the same people regularly over their adult years. After the first-generation subjects of the study began passing away, the researchers contacted their family members. A detailed record was kept of each individual and how he or she changed during the study.

The study found overwhelmingly that relationships are better indicators of happiness, health, and longevity than social class, IQ, income, or even genes. The study found very little relationship between how long a person's parents or other ancestors lived and how long the individual lived. Social relationships were a far better indicator. According to the Harvard study, satisfaction with relationships at fifty was the best predictor of how people were going to grow old. Those who were most satisfied with relationships at fifty were the healthiest at eighty.[3]

Having close relationships is the key factor. You need a few people you are close to and with whom you can share things that are important to you and even things that aren't too important. Building on the Harvard Study, Wes Moss found that at least three close connections beyond your spouse is the benchmark. Fewer than three close relationships can be an indicator of unhappiness in retirement.

The importance of relationships in retirement was hammered home in a meta-analysis in which the researchers compared many published studies. After aggregating results, they concluded that stronger social relationships increased the likelihood of survival by 50 percent, estimating that loneliness or social isolation had an effect on health and longevity equivalent to smoking fifteen cigarettes per day.[4]

Staying married to the same person (whether a first or second spouse) also improves your outlook on life, as well as your physical and mental health. The Harvard Study found that people with happy marriages had consistently better moods that didn't decline even on days when they were experiencing pain.

In another vein of research, generally known as the Blue Zone studies, Dan Buettner identified different regions in the world where the residents lived longer than those in the rest of the world, which he called Blue Zones. Buettner sought to identify habits and practices that were common to the Blue Zones. One characteristic common to these areas is that people in those places had relationships with other people who practiced healthy lifestyles, something that made a person more likely to adopt a healthy lifestyle and benefit from it.[5]

In his surveys, Wes Moss found that visiting a social epicenter at least once a week greatly improved happiness. He defined an epicenter as a place where multiple people gathered. It can be a place of worship, social or golf group, senior center, neighborhood group, or charitable group. The gathering can be formal or informal.[6]

The lesson is clear and simple. Relationships are vital to a happy and successful retirement, as well as to health and longevity. After working on your finances, work on your relationships and continue working on them through retirement.

Take Care of Your Body

Taking care of your body improves physical and mental health and significantly reduces the stress of retirement.

The Harvard Study emphasizes a few healthy lifestyle factors as critical to a longer and healthier life. Not smoking or abusing alcohol top the list. Next is engaging in physical activity. Related to that is maintaining a healthy body weight.

The Blue Zone studies founds that diet is important and that several types of diets are beneficial. You don't have to follow an extreme diet; you can find a diet that is both healthy and that appeals to you. Read about the Blue Zone diets and other healthy eating practices to discover an eating pattern that works for you.

An interesting finding of the Blue Zone studies is that you don't have to deprive yourself to the point of adopting an ascetic lifestyle. You don't have to abstain from alcohol or other pleasurable activities. In fact, the Blue Zone studies and some others found that moderate alcohol consumption seems to improve health and longevity.

Another interesting finding of the Blue Zone work is that a person shouldn't eat to fullness. Instead, eat only until you feel 80 percent full. Another finding was to avoid eating after the early evening. Eat the last meal of the day in late afternoon or early evening.

All the studies recommend physical activity, but not in the way you might expect. Extreme exercise isn't necessary and might even have negative effects. I's a good idea to avoid what's become a common practice in the U.S. and much of the Western world. Don't engage in an hour or so of strenuous exercise either early or late in the day and spend the rest of the day being sedentary. It's better to have some level of physical activity several times during the day. The Blue Zone research indicates that in addition to a daily exercise program, it's a good idea to try to be active during the day through regular activities. In other words, develop some hobbies and activities that require movement, such as gardening, playing golf, or walking. The Pritikin Center for Health and Longevity recommends two exercise sessions a day, a full workout in the morning and lighter exercise later in the day, such as a walk.[7]

Taking care of your body includes incorporating activities that reduce stress. This is important, because reducing stress reduces inflammation, which is now considered to be a key trigger for a number of diseases and chronic conditions. The best stress-reduction activities vary by individual. For some people, exercise and social activities reduce stress. Other people benefit from activities such as prayer, meditation, and napping. You need to determine the stress-reduction activities that work for you.

Create Purpose and Identity

Having purpose is important. People are generally goal oriented. They need a reason to wake up in the morning, get out of bed, and put on some clothes. Many people don't even realize until after retiring the sense of purpose that work gave them. For these people, and those whose identity is tied to their work, leaving work can be costly.

Many people become depressed or engage in unhealthy habits after retiring because they haven't replaced the purpose and identity that work gave them.

In addition, work often stimulates our curiosity. We keep exploring and learning new things to stay on top of changes at our work and be good at our jobs. After retiring, it's important not to lose our curiosity. The desire to learn new things and actually learning new things are two qualities that help maintain mental health and reduce cognitive decline as we age.[8]

You don't need one big thing to establish purpose and identity in retirement. In fact, most successful retirees have multiple activities.

Wes Moss found in his surveys that the happiest retirees had more than three of what he calls "core pursuits."

These pursuits don't need to be serious activities the way work was. They can be hobbies and other leisure pursuits. Travel, family activities, and sports can replace what was lost by leaving work. For many successful retirees, volunteer activities fulfill much of their purpose and identity. Successful retirees who engage in multiple volunteer activities aren't unusual.

Relationships can be important contributors to your purpose and identity. It takes a lot of work to establish and maintain quality relationships, whether the relationships are with family or friends. That way you can accomplish two important goals with one set of actions.

Aging Is a State of Mind

"You're as young as you feel" and similar sayings are often used to encourage people to change their attitudes about life and growing older. *Breaking the Age Code* by Becca Levy combines research and anecdotes to make the case that people should take those sayings to heart.

Levy combined data from the Ohio Longitudinal Study on Aging and Retirement with data from the National Death Index to gauge how attitudes about aging affect lifespans. Levy's conclusion is that people with the most positive views about aging outlived those with the most negative views by 7.5 years.

Levy reviewed other studies showing that memory lapses don't have to be a part of aging and that attitudes about aging are a major factor in retaining cognitive abilities. Those with positive attitudes about aging outperform others on memory tests.

Levy argues that many health problems formerly considered to be entirely due to the aging process, such as memory loss, hearing decline, and cardiovascular events, are instead influenced by the negative beliefs about aging dominant in the United States and other developed countries.

Levy, disagreeing with those who believe that seniors with positive attitudes about aging are those who've been fortunate enough to have better health as they aged, concludes that positive attitudes about aging improve health.[9]

Plan for Retirement Success

Just as important as, and perhaps more important than, a financial plan, is a plan for the nonfinancial aspects of retirement. You must answer the big question: How will I spend my time? Another important and related question to ask is: What makes me happy?

Consider how you'll spend typical days and what you'll do during most weeks. Try to determine the seasonal activities you'll take part in during certain months of the year.

One of my longtime subscribers once told me that a reason he subscribed to Retirement Watch for years was that I reminded readers that a successful retirement is work. It's not an endless vacation or string of Saturdays. You must be active and stay active, both mentally and physically. Most of us need a plan to make the nonfinancial aspects of retirement successful, and that plan needs to be revised on a regular basis during retirement.

NOTES

Chapter 1: The Coming Retirement Squeeze: Why the Mid-2020s Will Be a Tough Time for Many Retirees

1. The Board of Trustees, Federal Hospital Insurance and Federal Supplementary Medical Insurance Trust Funds, 2022 Annual Report, https://www.cms.gov/files/document/2022-medicare-trustees-report.pdf.

Chapter 3: Why You Need Guaranteed Lifetime Income to Reduce Risk and Increase Spending

1. John Ameriks, Robert Veres, Mark J. Warshawsky, "Making Retirement Income Last a Lifetime," *Journal of Financial Planning*, January 2001, https://papers.ssrn.com/sol3/papers.cfm?abstract_id=292259. The study is discussed in Wade Pfau, "'Making Retirement Income Last a Lifetime,'" Retirement Researcher, https://retirementresearcher.com/making-retirement-income-last-a-lifetime/.

2. Wade Pfau, "A Broader Framework for Determining an Efficient Frontier for Retirement Income," *Journal of Financial Planning*, February 2013.

3. Wade Pfau, "Why Bond Funds Don't Belong in Retirement Portfolios," Advisor Perspectives, August 4, 2015, https://www.advisorperspectives.com/articles/2015/08/04/why-bond-funds-don-t-belong-in-retirement-portfolios.

4. David M. Blanchett, "The Impact of Guaranteed Income and Dynamic Withdrawals on Safe Initial Withdrawal Rates," *Journal of Financial Planning* 2 (April 2017), https://www.financialplanningassociation.org/article/journal/APR17-impact-guaranteed-income-and-dynamic-withdrawals-safe-initial-withdrawal-rates.

5. Pfau, "Why Bond Funds Don't Belong."

6. David Blanchett and Michael S. Finke, "Guaranteed Income: A License to Spend," Social Science Research Network, June 28, 2021, https://papers.ssrn.com/sol3/papers.cfm?abstract_id=3875802.

7. Pfau, "A Broader Framework." See also Pfau, "Why Bond Funds Don't Belong."

8. Blanchett and Finke, "Guaranteed Income."

Chapter 4: Don't Leave Money on the Table: How to Make the Most of Social Security

1. Matt Fellowes et al.,"The Retirement Income Solution Hiding In Plain Sight," United Income, June 28, 2019, https://davidlukasfinancial.com/wp-content/uploads/2021/09/UI_Social_Security_White_Paper.pdf.

2. The Harris Poll, "Social Security Consumer Survey," Nationwide Retirement Institute, July 2020, https://mutualfunds.nationwide.com/media/pdf/NFM-19602AO.pdf.

3. For more details about how to qualify for Social Security and how benefits are computed, see Robert Carlson, *Where's My Money?*

Secrets to Getting the Most out of Your Social Security (Regnery Capital: 2021).

4. William Meyer and William Reichenstein, "How the Social Security Claiming Decision Affects Portfolio Longevity," *Financial Planning Journal* (April 2012), https://www.financialplanningassociation.org/article/how-social-security-claiming-decision-affects-portfolio-longevity.

5. Ibid.

Chapter 6: The Spending Plan: Why It's Critical, and How Most Retirement Plans Get It Wrong

1. See "Estimating Changes in Retirement Expenditures and the Retirement Spending Smile," Kitces.com, April 30, 2014, https://www.kitces.com/blog/estimating-changes-in-retirement-expenditures-and-the-retirement-spending-smile/ for much of the key research based on the DOL data.

2. Anne Tergeson, "Cut Your Spending, Says Creator of the 4% Rule," *Wall Street Journal*, April 19, 2022, https://www.wsj.com/articles/cut-your-retirement-spending-now-says-creator-of-the-4-rule-11650327097?mod=hp_featst_pos4.6

3. Elizabeth Arias and Jiaquan Xu, "United States Life Tables, 2019," Centers for Disease Control, March 22, 2022, https://www.cdc.gov/nchs/data/nvsr/nvsr70/nvsr70-19.pdf.

Chapter 7: How to Avoid the Mistakes Most People Make about Medicare and Retirement Medical Expenses

1. "Cost of Health Care: A New Way to Calculate Retirement Health Care Costs," T. Rowe Price, March 29, 2022, https://www

.troweprice.com/personal-investing/resources/insights/a-new-way-to
-calculate-retirement-health-care-costs.html#:~:text=According
%20to%20T.%20Rowe%20Price%E2%80%99s%20Retirement
%20Savings%20and,health%20insurance%20premiums%2C
%20and%20out-of-pocket%20health%20care%20expenses.1.

2. "Living in the COVID-19 Pandemic: The Health, Finances, and Retirement Prospects of Four Generations: 21st Annual Transamerica Retirement Survey of Workers," Transamerica Center for Retirement Studies, August 2021, https://transamericacenter.org/docs/default -source/retirement-survey-of-workers/tcrs2021_sr_four-generations -living-in-a-pandemic.pdf.

3. Paul Fronstin and Jack VanDerhei, "Savings Medicare Beneficiaries Need for Health Expenses in 2019: Some Couples Could Need as Much as $363,000," Employee Benefit Research Institute, May 16, 2019, https://www.ebri.org/health/publications/issue-briefs/content /summary/savings-medicare-beneficiaries-need-for-health-expenses -in-2019.

4. "Fidelity Releases 2022 Retiree Health Care Cost Estimate: 65-Year-Old Couple Retiring Today Will Need an Average of $315,000 for Medical Expenses" (press release), Fidelity Investments, May 16, 2022, http://fidelityinvestments2020news.q4web.com/press-releases /news-details/2022/Fidelity-Releases-2022-Retiree-Health-Care -Cost-Estimate-65-Year-Old-Couple-Retiring-Today-Will-Need-an -Average-of-315000-for-Medical-Expenses/default.aspx.

5. Katy Votava and Cymantha M. Campbell, *Making the Most of Medicare: A Guide for Boomers* (Pittsford, New York: Goodcare Productions, LLC, 2020).

6. Juliette Cubanski et al., "How Much Do Medicare Beneficiaries Spend Out of Pocket on Health Care?," Kaiser Family Foundation, November 4, 2019, https://www.kff.org/medicare/issue-brief/how -much-do-medicare-beneficiaries-spend-out-of-pocket-on-health -care/.

7. Juliette Cubanski et al., "Medicare Beneficiaries' Out-of-Pocket Healthcare Spending as a Share of Income Now and Projections for the Future," Kaiser Family Foundation, January 26, 2018, https:// www.kff.org/report-section/medicare-beneficiaries-out-of-pocket -health-care-spending-as-a-share-of-income-now-and-projections -for-the-future-report.

Chapter 8: Who Will Change My Light Bulbs? How to Sort through the Confusion and Chaos in Long-Term Care

1. "Genworth Study Reveals American Would Rather Go to the Dentist Than Talk about Their Long Care Planning and Aging Needs," Genworth Financial, November 13, 2014, https://www.prnewswire .com/news-releases/genworth-study-reveals-americans-would-rather -go-to-the-dentist-than-talk-about-their-long-term-care-planning -and-aging-needs-282599291.html.

2. Alexandra Olson, "Retirement Planning Should Include Long-Term Care Costs," *USA Today*, November 17, 2017, https://www.usatoday .com/story/money/personalfinance/retirement/2017/11/17/retirement -planning-should-include-long-term-care-costs/866344001/.

3. "Long-Term Care Insurance Facts—Data—Statistics—2022 Reports," American Association for Long-Term Care Insurance, 2022, https://www.aaltci.org/long-term-care-insurance/learning -center/ltcfacts-2022.php#total-claims-2022.

4. Ibid.

5. "Cost of Care Survey," Genworth, June 2, 2022, https://www .genworth.com/aging-and-you/finances/cost-of-care.html.

6. "Long-Term Care Insurance Facts."

Chapter 9: IRAs and 401(k)s: Maximizing the After-Tax Value of Your Most Valuable Assets

1. "Balancing Retirement Income, the Impact of Taxes, and the Potential to Build a Legacy," Allianz Life Insurance Company of North America, https://www.allianzlife.com/-/media/files/allianz /pdfs/newsroom/fact-sheet-rmd.pdf?msclkid=1eb902b9d15311ecbe 00f0a67bc3490d.

2. David Phillips and Todd Phillips, "The Bombshell Battle Plan: How to Defend against the IRS's Secret Weapon," Estate Planning Specialists, 2020, http://epmez.com/TheBombshellBattlePlan.pdf.

Chapter 10: The Five Big Retirement Tax Ambushes and How to Avoid Them

1. Patrick J. Purcell, "Income Taxes on Social Security Benefits," Social Security Administration, December 2015, https://www.ssa.gov /policy/docs/issuepapers/ip2015-02.html.

Chapter 11: Ensure Your Legacy: Estate Planning Is Much More than Tax Reduction

1. R. Sean Morrison et al., "What's Wrong with Advance Care Planning," *Journal of the American Medical Association* 326, no. 16 (October 8, 2021): 1575–76, https://jamanetwork.com/journals /jama/article-abstract/2785148.

Chapter 12: The Overlooked Retirement Asset: Making the Most of Your Home Equity

1. Elizabeth Ecker, "Majority of Baby Boomers Plan to Move for Retirement," Senior Housing News, March 25, 2014, https://staging. seniorhousingnews.com/2014/03/25/majority-of-baby-boomers-plan-to-move-for-retirement/; Amy Baxter, "Where Baby Boomers Plan to Move during Retirement," Home Health Care News, September 6, 2016, https://homehealthcarenews.com/2016/09/where-baby-boomers-plan-to-move-during-retirement/.

2. See, for example, Wade Pfau, *How to Use Reverse Mortgages to Secure Your Retirement* (Retirement Researcher Media, 2022).

Chapter 13: The Solo Years: When Many Retirement Plans Fail

1. For a more detailed discussion of life expectancy, see Robert Carlson, *Where's My Money?: Secrets to Getting the Most Out of Your Social Security* (Regnery Capital: Washington, D.C., 2021).

Chapter 14: Do Retirees Have Too Much Invested in Stocks? (and Other Investment Issues)

1. Wade Pfau, *Retirement Planning Guidebook* (Retirement Researcher Media, 2021).

2. Robert C. Carlson, *The New Rules of Retirement* (Hoboken, New Jersey: Wiley, 2004)

3. Craig L. Israelsen, *7Twelve: A Diversified Investment Portfolio with a Plan* (Hoboken, New Jersey: Wiley, 2010); Alex Shahidi, *Balanced Asset Allocation: How to Profit in Any Economic Climate* (Hoboken, New Jersey: Wiley, 2015).

4. Wade Pfau and Michael Kitces, "Reducing Retirement Risk with a Rising Equity Glidepath," *Journal of Financial Planning*, January 2014.

Chapter 15: How to Avoid the Major Causes of Retirement Failure and Achieve True Success in Retirement

1. "Life Stress Self Assessment: The Holmes and Rahe Stress Scale," Justice Institute of British Columbia, https://www.jibc.ca/sites/default /files/community_social_justice/pdf/cl/Life_Stress_Self_Assessment _(Holmes_and_Rahe).pdf.

2. Wes Moss, *What the Happiest Retirees Know* (New York: McGraw Hill, 2021).

3. For details of the Harvard Study, see George E. Vaillant, *Aging Well* (New York: Little, Brown Spark, 2003) and the TED Talk by Robert Waldinger, "What Makes a Good Life."

4. Julianne Holt-Lunstad et al., "Social Relationships and Mortality Risk: A Meta-Analytic Review," *PLOS Medicine*, July 27, 2010, https:// journals.plos.org/plosmedicine/article?campaign_id=9&emc=edit _nn_20220507&id=10.1371%2Fjournal.pmed.1000316&instance _id=60757&nl=the-morning&regi_id=5778985&segment_id= 91601&te=1&user_id=222a55becba78122d318d31bbfc12d9c.

5. Dan Buettner, *The Blue Zones: 9 Lessons for Living Longer from the People Who've Lived the Longest*, 2nd ed. (National Geographic, 2012).

6. Moss, *What the Happiest Retirees Know.*

7. Robert Pritikin, *The New Pritikin Program* (New York: Gallery Books, 2007).

8. Guy McKhann and Marilyn Albert, *Keep Your Brain Young* (Hoboken, New Jersey: Wiley, 2002).

9. Becca Levy, *Breaking the Age Code: How Your Beliefs About Aging Determine How Long and Well You Live* (New York: HarperCollins, 2021).

INDEX